WRITE YOUR COZY MYSTERY

A PRACTICAL HOW-TO GUIDE

RACHEL WARD

WRITE YOUR COZY *mystery*

A practical How-To-Guide

RACHEL WARD

COZY PRESS

CONTENTS

Write Your Cozy Mystery: A Practical How-To Guide

Copyright Rachel Ward (2024)

ISBN 978-1-0685077-0-0

Published by Cozy Books.

Requests to publish work from this book should be sent to inf@rachelwardbooks.com

www.rachelwardbooks.com

*Dedicated with thanks, to the dear family and friends
who have supported my writing journey
over the years.*

1
OUTLINE

ozy mysteries are selling like hot cakes. This book will guide you through the steps you'll need to think about the cozy mystery that YOU could write, help you to prepare the ground and then tackle your first draft.

ABOUT ME

'Rachel is an amazing storyteller. I love her book and characters. They seem so real.'
— Amazon customer, review, 22.10.22

I've been a professional author since 2009, starting with young adult (YA) novels and then moving to psychological thrillers and cozy mysteries. I also teach creative writing, provide mentoring and run a monthly chat on Twitter/X (#CosyCrimeClub). My YA book, Numbers, won many regional book awards, was shortlisted for the prestigious Waterstones Children's Book Prize, sold to twenty-six countries and was optioned for film. The first four books in my cozy series, the Supermarket Mysteries published by Joffe Books, all hit the Top 20 Cozy Mystery chart on Amazon in the UK. They feature amateur detective, Bea, who is a smart checkout girl in a fictional supermarket, Costsave, and her friend Ant, the streetwise trainee. Set in a small English town, the books cover contemporary issues with a light touch, along with a decent smattering of murder and intrigue.

I started to write cozy crime at a time in my life when writing provided a welcome escape from the real world. In doing so, I rediscovered my joy in writing and I created characters who have become like old friends. Every time I start a new Supermarket Mystery, it feels like reconnecting with people I know and love.

I suspect many people who read cozy mysteries are looking for that escape too, and it is a pleasure and a privilege to write the sort of stories that provide comfort.

I'm writing this from the perspective of an English author of mystery books set in the UK. Although my books have sold in many territories, I'm most familiar with the UK book market. I'll be using the US spelling 'cozy' throughout as this is becoming the internationally accepted term for the genre.

3

ABOUT YOU

*'Stay afraid, but do it anyway. What's important is the
action. You don't have to wait to be confident. Just do it
and eventually the confidence will follow.'*
— Carrie Fisher

There may be all sorts of reasons why you have selected this book. You may be new to writing or an established writer trying a new genre. You may have started writing your cozy mystery already or just have an idea that won't leave you alone. Perhaps you are grabbing ten minutes here and there to write around your other commitments (I've been there!) or have cleared the decks for a few months to write a novel. Whatever your background and experience, this book will give you the tools you need to write a cozy mystery that hooks your readers and gives them the equivalent of a hug in a book.

One thing that you must bring is a love of the genre. A book takes a long time to complete from first idea to finished draft. You have to live with your characters and their predicaments for months, even years, and you have to love spending time in their company. If you have a passion for reading cozy mysteries, this will shine through in your writing and your readers will love your stories. You will also learn so much from other writers: subject matter, character development, plotting. It's all there to be absorbed, as you develop your own writing style.

New writers are often told to 'write what you know.' I say 'write what you love.'

If you love this genre but are new to writing, you may have a little voice in your head asking, 'Can I write a cozy mystery? Can I really do it?' The answer is emphatically 'yes' and you will find out how in this step-by-step guide which will give you the confidence to start, persist and finish your cozy mystery. Let's get going!

THE RISE OF THE COZY MYSTERY

'Crime fiction confirms our belief, despite some evidence to the contrary, that we live in a rational, comprehensible, and moral universe.'
— P.D. James

While detective fiction has its origins in Wilkie Collins' The Moonstone and, of course, Conan Doyle's Sherlock Holmes books, it is the crime fiction of the 1920s and 30s, known as the Golden Age of Detective Fiction, which is the real precursor of modern cozy crime writing. During this period, Agatha Christie created two of the most famous and enduring amateur detectives of all time – Miss Marple and Hercule Poirot – while Dorothy L. Sayers introduced her aristocratic detective Lord Peter Wimsey and his companion, Harriet Vane. Other authors, like Josephine Tey and Freeman Wills Croft featured police detectives, but it is the idea of the amateur sleuth which has been picked up by modern writers.

Often these novels were framed as a puzzle, which the reader was invited to try and solve along with the detective, winnowing the real clues from the red herrings. In the end, justice was seen to be done, although sometimes the murderer took their own way out instead of facing the consequences of a trial, and, in those days in the UK, capital punishment.

It's only recently that these books have been described as 'cosy crime' or 'cozy mysteries', although exactly how 'cozy' they really are is up for debate. Certainly, Christie's books contain some very dark drama and the worst of human nature.

In the 1980s, 90s and 2000s, writers MC Beaton and Alexander McCall Smith flew the flag for gentler mysteries. McCall Smith's first book in his The No 1 Ladies Detective Agency series was published in 1998 and the series has sold over 20 million copies in the English language.

The most recent surge in cozy mystery sales, in

the UK and increasingly elsewhere, has been spear-headed by Richard Osman's The Thursday Murder Club series. In an interview with the BBC, Osman said, "When I started writing The Thursday Murder Club, the successful crime books of the time were mainly dark psychological thrillers with unreliable narrators. I just wanted to write an Agatha Christie-style thriller but with some humour and with a modern twist. A book I'd love to read, but couldn't find. I'd never heard the term 'cosy crime'."

Osman's books have been a publishing phenomenon. His fourth book in the series, The Last Devil to Die, was reported as selling over 140,000 hardback copies in its first week. The series deals with all sorts of issues not traditionally touched by cozy books – drug dealing, dementia, etc. – and he has shown that you can combine serious contempo-rary issues with an absorbing crime plot in an engaging way.

Steph Carey, Senior Commissioning Editor at Bonnier Books, and based in the UK, says that she is seeing two strands in cozy mysteries: the traditional, village mystery in an English village or small town, with a well-off or comfortably retired protagonist, and what she calls 'contemporary cozy' set in bigger towns or cities with a less old-fashioned feel.

In the USA, cozy mysteries have tended to live at the more whimsical end of the scale, featuring animals, baking or arts and crafts. An example of a long-running successful series is Lilian Jackson Braun's The Cat Who... mystery books which centre around journalist Jim Qwilleran and his two Siamese cats. While these sub-genre books are still going strong, more recently, the US has seen that the 'genre has begun shedding its protective cocoon, tackling the kinds of real-world struggles that many of its readers may have come to the books to escape: prejudice, financial insecurity, mental illness...' (according to Alyse Burnside, writing in The Atlantic).

If you are embarking on writing your own cozy mystery, you have an increasingly wide field to operate in, and your book can reflect your experiences, preferences, humour and background. Whatever angle you choose, this is a great time to be writing cozy mysteries as their popularity is riding high.

4.1 EXERCISES

1. Compile a list of your 'Top Five Cozy Mysteries'. Is there something that they all have in common? What do you like about them? List five elements that you look for in the books you most enjoy.

2. Do you only read one sort of mystery book? Challenge yourself to read out of your normal lane. For example, if you read contemporary mysteries, try an Agatha Christie. If you usually read books by UK authors, try a writer from the USA, and vice versa.

WHY ARE COZY MYSTERIES SO POPULAR?

'Cozies bring order to a world that is currently very chaotic.'
— Margaret Louden

In a world of social media, 24-hour news, climate change and political volatility, it is not a surprise that readers seek respite in a warm, predictable world where good triumphs over evil and people care about each other. Comfort-reading doesn't mean that we don't take world issues seriously, but that we all find our own way of processing worrying things and protecting our mental health. Regardless of the wider context, personal crises and tricky situations arise in every life – it's just part of being human – and books that provide an escape are often much treasured. A cozy mystery may feature murder, which in ordinary life would be upsetting, but the reader knows that by the end of the book, the case will be solved and closure reached. Each book provides the reader with one or two crimes which they know can and will be resolved.

During the pandemic, many people sought refuge in books. In fact, in the UK sales of all print books rose by 5% compared to the previous year, with fiction up 20% from 2 years before, propelled by 19% volume growth for crime and thrillers, 23% for science fiction and fantasy, and 49% for romance. 'Overall, the year's bestsellers show book buyers seeking out comfort, laughter, escapism, familiarity and maybe a sense of community...' said Nielson Bookscan's Jackie Swope.

I wrote the first draft of The Missing Checkout Girl, which started my Supermarket Mysteries series, when my husband was very ill. I had publishing woes, too, as I was waiting to find out if a publisher wanted a young adult novel which I had rewritten several times (spoiler alert – they didn't). In the middle of all this, I discovered a cast of characters which lifted me out of my prevailing gloom and worry. I got caught up in their story, and shared it chapter by chapter with my husband, emailing it to his Kindle when he had an extended hospital stay. I get emotional thinking about now, because it was such a special thing to be able to do, and I can honestly say that this book helped us both through a very difficult time. Words are powerful, make no mistake about that, and good-hearted story can have as much impact as a dark one.

Alexander McCall Smith's website invites you to 'Find happiness within the pages of an Alexander McCall Smith book' which, I think goes some way to explaining the popularity of cozy mysteries. For centuries, people have enjoyed escaping into the pages of a book, and with cozy mysteries, we are providing stories that people can get wrapped up in – the crime-writing world's equivalent of a hug.

5.1 EXERCISES

1. Write down five adjectives which describe
   the feeling you want to give readers when
   they spend time with your book. Think
   about how you want them to feel when

they pick it up, as they read it and then after they finish the last page.

2. Think about one of your favourite books. What sort of 'reading journey' does it take you on? Write down the feelings you can remember experiencing the first time you read it.

6

THE ESSENTIAL ELEMENTS OF A COZY MYSTERY

'And there are rules for crime fiction. Or if not rules, at least expectations and you have to give the audience what it wants.'
— Tod Goldberg

While the range of books which can be considered 'cozy' seems to be expanding rapidly, from the very mild and gentle to edgier stories dealing with contemporary issues, there are common factors which readers will expect in our books.

- Amateur detectives (for the most part. We will explore detectives in Chapter Nine.)

- No graphic violence
- Little or no sex
- A cast of likeable characters
- A satisfying ending

6.1 NO GRAPHIC VIOLENCE OR FORENSIC DETAIL

While cozy mysteries usually contain a murder or two (although other crimes can and do feature) violence is kept off screen, and writers do not dwell on the forensic state of any bodies found. Although, as we have seen, cozy mysteries are a broad church these days, this is probably the one cardinal rule which they all follow.

6.2 LITTLE OR NO SEX

Traditionally, there has been no romance and certainly no sex in cozy mystery books. This, too, is changing with one sub-genre of cozy mysteries featuring a strong romance thread. Again, there are ways and ways of dealing with this, and for the most part, any sex is hinted at rather than seen.

6.3 A CAST OF LIKEABLE CHARACTERS

People who read cozy mysteries do so as much for the returning cast of characters as for the crime aspect. As Simon Cowell used to say on TV's The X Factor, it's all about 'likeability.' As a writer, it is worth working on this until you feel you've got it right. It doesn't mean your characters have to be perfect. On the contrary, readers are happy for your characters to have relatable flaws and idiosyncrasies, but our amateur detectives tend not to be the more broken or damaged souls to be found in police procedurals, noir books of various sorts or psychological thrillers.

6.4 A SATISFYING ENDING

Whatever we put our characters through, our readers will pick up our books knowing that justice will prevail at the end. Our amateur detectives will use their guile, knowhow, contacts and courage to puzzle out whodunnit and make sure that they don't get away with it. In some, edgier crime books loose ends may not be tied up quite so firmly, and there is sometimes ambiguity over the consequences of crime for the criminal. In a cozy mystery, order is restored by the final chapter and the reader is left with a feeling of satisfaction, security and a desire to find out what our detectives get up to next.

6.5 EXERCISES

1. Can you remember the five elements of a cozy mystery described in this chapter? Can you relate these to your favourite cozy mysteries? Do any of your favourite books break the 'rules' and do they make that work?

2. As a reader, which of the elements do you think is most important or do they have equal value?

7

HOW COZY IS COZY? IS ANYTHING OFF LIMITS?

'Your favourite cake in a book... it's so delicious that you can't help yourself returning to get another slice.'
— 'Kindle Customer', Amazon review, The Missing Babysitter Mystery, 7/10/23

Contemporary cozy mystery books range from very 'safe' to slightly edgy. One thing you might want to decide fairly early on is where your writing fits on this scale. This will help you to shape your characters, plot and tone.

If you are aiming for the softer end of the market, then you really can't be too cozy. These books are more formulaic and your readers are not looking for any shocks or surprises. Focus instead on gentle humour, a satisfying mystery element, and characters that your readers will enjoy spending time with. Obviously, you will be keeping any violence implied and off screen, but there are some other things which you should definitely steer clear of – gangs, organised crime, drugs, modern slavery, sexual assault, etc. If your suspects are caught up in a plot involving stolen goods, think about antique books or a precious jewel, rather than a suitcase full of heroin. Most cozy mysteries tend to avoid subjects which involve the grubbier or more unappealing side of life.

For books at the edgier end of the scale, you can include most topics but it must be done with the lightest of touches. Richard Osman does have drug dealers in his fourth book, but the tone of his writing and the characterisation of his villains means that this works in a book which is still firmly cozy. Dark subjects can be tackled but you don't want to give your reader nightmares.

7.1 EXERCISES

1. Where on the scale of safe to edgy do you want your book to sit? If you think of a scale of 0 to 10, with 0 as the safest and 10 as the edgiest, where are you aiming for with yours?

2. If you are planning on including contemporary or edgy themes, think about how you might do this in a cozy setting. Can you think of examples where similar themes have been covered in a book that you have read? How did the author tackle this?

8

HOW DO YOU GET STARTED?

'Everybody walks past a thousand story ideas every day.
The good writers are the ones who see five or six of them.
Most people don't see any.'
— Orson Scott Card

There are many different ways of working. None of them is 'right' – you have to find what works for you. I will give you some ideas and can tell you what has worked for me. I have had twelve books published (and several rejected) and have used a variety of methods. Although I'm sorry to say that I haven't discovered one surefire approach which will always work, I have assembled a wide range of methods, tools and tricks which I can call on when the going gets tough.

In reality, each new book seems like a mountain to climb and in setting out to write a book, you have to accept that it is a big commitment in terms of time, energy and focus. Some mountains are steeper than others. You won't always get to the top. Sometimes you veer off track, or there's a landslip which is out of your control and cuts your journey short or necessitates a long diversion. The important thing is to enjoy the adventure!

So, when we're surveying a distant mountain range of ideas in our minds, how do we get started? How do we decided which peak is the one to commit to. How do we even come up with ideas? In truth, a story can start anywhere…

8.1 WHERE DO YOU GET YOUR IDEAS?

I used to do a lot of school visits to promote my YA books. One question which was always asked was 'Where do you get your ideas from?'

In one way, it is unanswerable. I believe that our brains produce ideas from the 'soup' of all our experiences and influences, including:

- Life Experiences
- News stories
- Films, books, TV shows
- Art exhibitions
- Overheard conversations
- People you know well or who you have glimpsed on the street
- Places which are special to us

This quote from Brooke Hampton, a US author sums it up rather beautifully. 'I am pieces of all the places I have been, and the people I have loved. I've been stitched together by song lyrics, book quotes, adventure, late night conversations, moonlight and the smell of coffee.'

Remember, your experience is gold to be mined. What might appear humdrum to you could be unusual to others or perhaps it will strike a chord. For example, my Supermarket Mysteries feature a setting which is familiar to nearly everyone with details which readers can relate to. I have had some wonderful messages from people who have worked in similar stores or whose family members do.

You may have experience of a work setting which gives you insider knowledge and would be fascinating to readers who are outside that world. The same may be true for your life experiences. The Mothers' Murder Club Mysteries by Kate Ailes feature an ante-natal group as detectives, drawing on the author's own experiences of meeting new people when expecting her first child. The Dinner Lady Detectives Series draws on author Hannah Hendy's catering experience. Your specialist knowledge and experience can bring authenticity and interest to a story.

You can also mine your emotions. You don't have to write directly about your own life experiences (grief, loss, disappointments, hope, joy, etc.), but you will naturally find yourself drawing on these feelings and memories as you put your characters through the mill. Don't be afraid to tap into these feelings. They are part of what makes you who you are – a unique writer telling your story.

8.2 IDEA-GENERATING TIPS

We can think of the brain as like a fruit machine, churning through all this information and occasionally spitting out random combinations of things which might work or might not. If you are having problems coming up with an idea that really grabs you, try one of these idea-generating tips.

- The most valuable question a writer can ask is 'What if?'

Take a news story that you've read, seen or heard and run with it. Ask yourself a range of 'What if?' questions and explore the story potential in the various options.

- Combinations

Some of the most successful books combine themes, topics, even genres – can you think of ways that you could bring together two things you care passionately about?

- People-watching/Eavesdropping

Take yourself off for a walk or to a café and observe (without staring or being weird!), then make up stories about the people you have seen. At one time in my life, I enlivened regular long, boring car journeys by wondering about the lives of people I would observe at motorway service stations. Who were they? Where were they travelling to? What was their relationship? In fact, this gave rise to a psychological thriller, The Girl Who Vanished, which was a pleasing example of making creative lemonade out of life's lemons.

- Keep an ideas notebook or file.

Jot down things as you think of them, even if it's just a one liner, a half-formed notion or snippet of conversation. Often, looking back through a notebook like this, old ideas will jump out at you. It sometimes takes a while for ideas to develop, for you to see how they fit with something else, or for you to be ready to write them in terms of your own emotional or psychological development. Sometimes, an idea is a great one, but its time hasn't yet come.

8.3 EXERCISES

1. Every day for a week, try coming up with
   three story ideas. Use the list in 8.1 as a
   prompt if you are struggling. Jot them
   down quickly and don't worry if they are

any good or not. Move on to the next one. See if it becomes easier as the week progresses.

2. Look at your list of ideas and mark the three strongest ones with an asterisk or highlighter. What makes them appeal to you? Why do they stand out?

9

CHARACTERS

'... liking the person we go on a journey with is the single most important element in drawing us into the story.'
— Blake Snyder

Your cozy mystery's success rests primarily on your main characters, who will be a likeable detective team and whose relationships have potential to develop through a series. So, let's get to know them.

9.1 HOW MANY DETECTIVES?

Your detectives will be at the heart of your book, and, hopefully, series, so getting them right from the start is important. Although Agatha Christie created enduring solo detectives in the form of Hercule Poirot and Miss Marple, I'm struggling to think of a modern cozy mystery where one amateur sleuth solves crime in splendid isolation. For the sake of plot development, the mechanics of an investigation, the potential to bring warmth and to allow scope for the evolution of a series of books, we really need two or more detectives.

I picked two main characters for my Supermarket Mysteries, Ant and Bea, and bring in others from my staple cast when they are needed. Alexander McCall Smith's iconic and long-running series, The No 1 Ladies Detective Agency, features Mma Ramotswe and her assistant Grace Makutsi. Julia Chapman's Dales Detectives series has Samson O'Brien and Delilah Metcalfe in the lead roles and the series tracks their changing relationship. In S.J. Bennett's Her Majesty Investigates series, The Queen is the main and unchanging protagonist, of course, but the legwork of the investigations is done by her Private Secretary, which for the first three books is Rozie Oshodi. In some books, the sidekick is an animal. For example, Vaseem Khan's Baby Ganesh Detective Agency books feature a little elephant. James

Runcie's Granchester books are slightly unusual in featuring an amateur detective, Sidney Chambers with a police partner, Detective Inspector Geordie Keating. It is more common to keep a useful contact (or foe) in the local police as one of the stock side characters.

With two main protagonists, there are many different potential dynamics. For example, you can have an unlikely friendship between people who on the surface don't seem to have much in common but then grow to like each other, a senior partner and a sidekick, or a romantic 'will they, won't they' plotline.

The relationship possibilities obviously expand the more detectives you have. In Peter Boland's Charity Shop Detective Agency series, the sleuths are three older women, who volunteer in a charity shop in a seaside town. Bella Ellis's Bronte Mysteries centre around the three Bronte sisters, who are reimagined as prototype 'detectors'.

The most successful cozy mystery series in the UK at the moment, Richard Osman's Thursday Murder Club series, features four residents in a retirement village which gives nice scope for bringing in different backstories and skills, developing relationships and so on.

9.2 WHAT DOES YOUR DETECTIVE DO?

Detectives in cozy mysteries are very rarely police officers themselves. There are some notable exceptions and in the UK we are seeing the popularity of police procedurals with a softer edge. For example, Mark Billingham's The Last Dance features Detective Declan Miller, and combines dark plotlines and seedy settings with laugh-out-loud humour. Elly Griffiths' Ruth Galloway series features a forensic archaeologist who works hand in hand with the police. For the most part, however, your detective will be an amateur, so what do they do?

Your detective will need plenty of time to pursue their investigation, as well as the potential to meet people and gain their trust. Again, think about how a series might develop. Someone working in too narrow a field might give you trouble in sustaining more than one book.

Retired people make wonderful amateur detectives in cozy mysteries, and there is a long line of them stretching back to Miss Marple herself. Both Richard Osman's Thursday Murder Club and Steph Broadribb's Retired Detectives Club feature four people in retirement complexes, and this has proved a winning formula. Retired people have plenty of time to give to their investigations, bring a wealth of experience and knowledge and are usually good at winkling information out of people.

Vaseem Khan, whose Baby Ganesh Detective Agency set in India features a retired police detective, said in an X/Twitter chat that I hosted (#cosycrimeclub), 'Police procedurals are great but amateur detectives can get away with more! Inspector Chopra retires in his late forties – he still has a policeman's instincts… so I get the best of both worlds.'

Of course, running a detective agency is a straightforward and handy way for a detective in a cozy mystery to earn a living. People bring cases to your door! You have contacts in the local community and the police. While not strictly 'amateur', there is no arguing that many successful cozy mysteries use such an agency as their basis. For example, Alexander McCall Smith's No 1 Ladies Detective Agency books or Julia Chapman's Dale Detective series.

Since 'cozy culinary mysteries' are an established sub-category, it makes perfect sense to think of food connections for your amateur detectives. Rosemary Shrager, herself a celebrated TV chef, writes about Prudence Bulstrode, a formidable freelance chef, in

The Last Supper and other books in the series. Orlando Murrin, food journalist, restauranteur and former Masterchef contestant features Peter Delamere, a charming but troubled chef in his debut novel, Knife Skills for Beginners. There are a multitude of cozy mysteries written in the USA and centred around cafes, restaurants and baking.

A common character in UK cozy mysteries is that of the detective vicar. Both James Runcie's Granchester Mysteries and the Reverend Richard Coles's Canon Clement Mysteries feature a practising priest as their protagonist, following in the tradition of G.K. Chesterton's Father Brown.

Retail workers are at the fore in my own Supermarket Mysteries and Peter Boland's Charity Shop Detectives Agency series. Other occupations in cozy mysteries include actor (the Charles Paris books by Simon Brett) and pub manager (Derek Farrell's Danny Bird Mysteries), hotel manager (Jean G. Goodhind's Honey Driver series set in a hotel in Bath), farmer (Kate Wells' Malvern Farm Mysteries series) and maid/cleaner (Nita Prose's bestselling series which starts with 'The Maid').

9.3 WHAT'S IN A NAME?

Names are important. Sometimes they can provide the key to a character. In cozy mysteries, you can have fun with names. Try out combinations of first names and surnames. Switch things around. If you are struggling, look up popular names from the year your character was born.

Embrace corny puns and word play! I have derived a lot of simple pleasure from my two detectives in the Supermarket Mysteries being called Ant and Bea, which harked back to a series of children's picture books which I loved when I was learning to read. Fiona Leitch's bestselling series features Jodie 'Nosey' Parker – the perfect name for an amateur sleuth. Julia Chapman's Dales Detective series star Samson O'Brien and Delilah Metcalfe.

Don't be afraid to change names in your quest to find the right one. I have often changed a character's name in the first, second or even third draft. Obviously, you need a very careful read through afterwards to check that you have substituted every single mention. In one novel, I swapped two characters' names, which was extremely confusing for my writing and editing brain. I wouldn't necessarily recommend that, but, in this case, it made for a better book in the end.

9.4 WHAT IS YOUR DETECTIVES' MOTIVATION FOR INVESTIGATING?

In the first book of a series, unless your detective is already an established crime-solver (like Dorothy L Sayers' Lord Peter Wimsey), you need to set out a reason for your protagonists to get involved in investigating the crime. Usually this is a personal one. For example, in the first of my Supermarket Mysteries – The Missing Checkout Girl Mystery – checkout worker Bea is angry that she doesn't feel safe walking home from work, after a customer and colleague are attacked. In book three, The Missing Babysitter Mystery, things are even closer to home as Bea's late father is revealed as the main suspect in a historic disappearance/murder and she wants to prove his innocence and clear his name. It might be that the victim is a friend or neighbour of your detective. Perhaps your detective is the person who discovers the first body. Take time to think why your detective is invested in this mystery. What are the stakes if they succeed or fail? Your detective needs to care about the outcome and your reader needs to care about them.

Vaseem Khan says of his character, Inspector Chopra, 'He has an old school sense of justice and I think that matters most,' which I believe is true of many of the best amateur detectives. They may have personal reasons for getting involved in investigating crimes, but they will also have a strong personal sense of right and wrong, fairness and justice.

9.5 WHY DON'T OUR DETECTIVES JUST LEAVE THINGS TO THE POLICE?

As writers, we need our detectives to take the lead in investigating crime, but it's important to establish why they don't just leave the police to it. There are a number of ways of dealing with this and you may find your own, but some scenarios are:

- They see the police either not being interested, not competent or over-worked/under-resourced.
- They feel they can go to places/ask questions the police may not be able to.

- Private detectives have people bringing cases to them, which can later develop into police matters.
- Sometimes the crime takes place in a remote place, so our amateur detective steps in until police can be called.

9.6 WHAT SKILLS DO THEY BRING?

While we invite our readers to empathise with our 'ordinary' detectives, it is useful to consider what particular skills and abilities our protagonists bring to their investigations. As you develop your characters, think about what would be helpful to your story and see if you can weave this in. If you have more than one main character, try to make their abilities complementary. For example, Bea Jordan in my Supermarket Mysteries is a secret maths whizz, which points to an analytical brain, useful in puzzling out mysteries, while her sidekick Ant is illiterate (at least at the start of book one) but has shown resourcefulness in masking this and finding ways around it. He also has all sorts of contacts among the dodgier members of the local community. When you are planning your characters, consider the following:

- Skills from existing/previous jobs.
- Personal qualities, for example, analytical brain, courage, inquisitiveness, ability to 'read' people, stubbornness.
- Social networks not accessible to the police.
- Ability to go under cover.
- Ability to observe in a detached manner, for example, the Queen in the Her Majesty Investigates books.

9.7 LIKEABILITY

Blake Snyder, a screenwriter, who has written an iconic (and extremely helpful) series of non-fiction writing books, the Save the Cat series, says, '... liking the person we go on a journey with is the single most important element in drawing us into the story.' He suggests writing a 'Save the Cat' scene when we meet the hero, in which they do something – like saving a cat – that defines who they are and makes us, the audience, like them. He quotes a hard-boiled thriller, Sea of Love, as his example. If this is true for harder-edged films and books, how much more important is likeability in a novel in which readers actively seek relatable characters that they can get to know over a series of books? As S.J. Bennett, the author of the Her Majesty Investigates series, says of Richard Osman's Thursday Murder Club detectives, 'We all want to be in their gang.'

With my Supermarket Mysteries, I've tried to portray a working environment where employees support each other and their community, and to make readers want to be part of the 'Costsave crew,' and happily that has happened for some!

'Love the characters, beautifully painted, folk just like people we know. I'd be a regular at till no. 6 if I lived in Kingsleigh!
– Stephen, Amazon review, The Missing Red Carpet Mystery, 30/12/23

9.8 OTHER CAST MEMBERS

Cozy mystery series usually involve a staple cast of side characters, as well as some who just feature in one book. Side characters can be very useful in contributing skills or contacts which your protagonists don't have. They can provide a welcome injection of humour if the plot is getting a little dark. New characters can be introduced more or less at any time. As your cast grows, it is worth keeping a record of names, ages, special characteristics or skills, for handy reference. A series bible is a file or collection of files recording the basic facts, characters, timelines and events for your books and we'll look a little closer at this in chapter 11.

9.9 EXERCISES (SUGGESTED 30 MINS EACH)

1. Fill in a character questionnaire for your main character(s) (sheet provided in 9.10 below). Feedback – did you find out anything unexpected about your detective(s)? Can you picture them more clearly now? Would it be useful to complete profiles for other characters in your book?

2. Interview your detective as if for a local newspaper, podcast or TV show at a pertinent point in your novel e.g. after a body has been discovered or after the crime has been solved. Put yourself in the shoes of the interviewer and find out about your

detective – Who are they? Where do they live? How/why did they get involved? What did they find out?

3. Write your character's name in the centre of a piece of paper and then map out their relationships to other people in the book – family, friends, colleagues, suspects.

9.10 CHARACTER QUESTIONNAIRE

Name:

Age:

Sex:

Physical Description:

Where do they live?

Who do they live with or do they live alone?

Describe your character's family relationships.

What is your character's attitude to their family?

What do they typically wear?

Favourite food?

Favourite TV programme/film?

Favourite book?

What is your character's education history?

What is your character's job?

What does your character like doing in their spare time?

What is your character's attitude to politics/current affairs?

What makes your character laugh?

What is your character's biggest regret?

Does your character have a secret?

What does your character hope for?

What is your character afraid of?

10

PLOT

'People misunderstand the purpose of storytelling structures. They're not 'Write these 11 scenes and you'll have a great story!' They're a foundation, a spine, a platform for you to build the rest of your story on top of.'
— Nathan Baugh, on X/Twitter

Any book needs a central thread that runs through it. With crime books, the crime or mystery is the thing and every scene/chapter must contribute to the progression of our protagonist's efforts to investigate it. It is the spine of the story.

10.1 THE TWO BASIC PLOT STRUCTURES IN COZY MYSTERIES

For cozy mysteries, the shape of the story, and the progression of the main plot will tend to take one of two well-trodden paths.

1. Murder at the beginning.

- Within the first 3 chapters: A murder
- At the mid-point: A second body or major incident
- End: Murderer is caught

This is the more usual format for contemporary cozy mystery books.

2. Murder in the Middle

- First half of book: The cast is introduced, which includes suspects, detective and victim(s)
- Mid-point: The first murder takes place
- Second half: The bodies pile up

- End: The detective gathers all suspects and reveals whodunnit.

This is familiar from numerous Agatha Christie books and others from the Golden Age of Crime-writing.

Of course you don't have to follow a well-trodden path, but I would advise it unless you are some sort of maverick writing genius (which you may well be!).

10.2 PLOTTING OR DISCOVERING?

Both basic structures provide a useful framework in which to develop your story. If you don't want to delve into the theoretical side of writing, that may be as much as you need. If you are happy with your concept, know the overall pattern your book is going to take and want to get on and write, then go for it! Many authors write their first draft without knowing whodunnit until they themselves approach the end.

There's no 'right' way to write a book and plenty of successful writers 'make things up as they go along' and used to be nicknamed 'pantsers' – people who write without a detailed outline 'by the seat of their pants.' This name is being replaced these days by the term 'discovery writer', someone who explores their book as they write a first draft or 'discovery draft.' I think I prefer this term. You are not rackety and random and just hoping things will work out somehow, instead you write to find out in the same way that your reader will read to find out – you are on the same journey.

If you are ready for your voyage of discovery, skip the next section, although bear in mind that you might want to come back to it later, if you get stuck. An understanding of structure can strengthen a book and help fix tricky editing problems.

If you suspect that you are a plotter, you will be following in the footsteps of Agatha Christie, who said, 'I think the real work is done in thinking out the development of your story and worrying about it until it comes right. That may take a while. Then, when you've got all your material together, all that remains is to find time to write the thing.'

10.3 UNDERSTANDING THE THEORY OF STORIES

If you feel that you would like more of a roadmap before you set out on your journey, there are plenty of plotting tools to help you develop this. In fact, the array of plotting methods out there can be rather overwhelming, and please don't let the weight of theory intimidate you or stifle your creativity. You may be the sort of person who writes well within a framework. You may just benefit from the extra knowledge, simmering away in the background of your brain, as you bring your story into the world. I will outline a few that I have found helpful and which illustrate some of the options available. As Delacroix said, apparently, 'First learn to be a craftsman; it won't keep you from being a genius.'

10.4 THREE ACT AND FIVE ACT STRUCTURES

The writing book which most writers recommend, and rightly so, is John Yorke's, Into the Woods. It's a scriptwriting book but works just as well for novels. In studying stories on the big and small screen, Yorke noticed 'an extraordinary uniformity' in stories. He states that 'storytelling has a shape that can be traced back to the beginnings of the recorded word. We absorb it.'

Rather reassuringly, he says, 'It's important to assert that writers don't need to understand structure. Many of the best have an uncanny ability to access story shape unconsciously,' but I have found that studying this a little does not take away the magic of writing, and, for some of my books, has been helpful in making a start or overcoming problems.

The three-act structure is 'the cornerstone of drama' in Western storytelling. It can be summarised as a beginning, a middle and an end, with turning points at the end of the first and second parts. Another way of putting this is a set up, then conflict and resolution with turning points at the inciting incident and the crisis. Please don't panic at this writing jargon – it's not as tricky as it sounds.

Shakespearean dramas and the Roman ones that came before them often use five acts. The five-act structure is really a refinement, expanding the second act into three, with the first and final acts staying the same. In the middle of the third act comes the midpoint – a development in the story which changes everything or in which something crucial is understood. Whatever has come before, nothing is the same after the mid-point.

I'm not suggesting that you have to create a table or spreadsheet and map out key plot points before you start, but some people will find this helpful. You can do this on a very basic level (a three-act structure showing a beginning, middle and end for your story and what happens at the 'tipping points' between acts), or you can work a great deal of detail into a five-act structure, perhaps having different rows in your table for key characters, or one row for each plot/sub-plot.

I will say, from experience, that it's important not to tie yourself up in knots over the theory of stories. You may not realise, but you already have an instinctive feel for the essential elements of a satisfying story.

10.5 SAVE THE CAT SCREENWRITING MODEL

Blake Snyder's 'Save the Cat' series of non-fiction books is another go to source for many writers.

Again, coming from a screenwriting background, Snyder is keen on you identifying the essence of your story and working from there. He has devised a useful fifteen point 'beat sheet' which he uses when pitching new projects. You fill in one or two lines for each beat to set out the course of your story. It does follow the overall pattern identified by Yorke, but his approach may suit you better.

10.6 THE SNOWFLAKE METHOD

'Good fiction doesn't just happen, it is designed,' says Randy Ingermanson, the creator of the Snowflake Method. He states that you can do the design work before or after you write your novel, but he strongly recommends the former. His idea stems from the way snowflakes form – you start small and build it up and his starting point is a one-sentence summary of the novel (like Blake Snyder's one-liner. Do you see a pattern here?). He suggests aiming for 15 words or fewer. It's worth spending quite a long time on this – it is the hook that will sell your book. If you meet a friend for coffee or happen to be travelling in a lift with a hotshot Hollywood producer, aim for one sentence that would answer the question, 'What's it about?'

Once you have one sentence that you are happy with, you expand this to a full paragraph describing the beginning, middle and end of your story. Ingermanson favours 'three disasters plus an ending' (which ties in with the three-act structure – disaster one at the end of Act 1, disaster two at the mid-point, disaster three at the end of Act 2). Then you develop a summary sheet for each of your main characters – listing their name, basic storyline, motivation, goal, conflict, epiphany and then a one-paragraph summary of their storyline. From here you go back to your original paragraph and expand each sentence into a paragraph, giving you a one-page synopsis of your novel. You continue on your merry way, expanding your character work, developing your storylines, even, he suggests, using a spreadsheet for this (I tend to use a Word file, but maybe I should be brave and try a spreadsheet).

I have found this approach incredibly helpful. I don't necessarily follow his steps slavishly, but the first few are such a good start for any new idea.

If you want to delve further into this, Ingermanson has free and paid for resources including a book and software. How To Write A Novel Using The Snowflake Method (advancedfictionwriting.com)

10.7 START IN THE MIDDLE

James Scott Bell's approach to tackling a novel is to start in the middle. In his book, 'Write Your Novel From The Middle' he explains the importance of the midpoint in a story. It is a fascinating exercise to open any book at the middle, to select 50% on a book on your Kindle, or to move the timer on a film on your TV to halfway through and see what is happening *at that precise point*. Bell's thesis is that this is a pivotal point and that it is possible to start from here when planning, using this crucial moment as a mirror marking when we move from pre-story state towards the ultimate transformation at the end. He also maintains that we need high stakes in a story, in order to make the reader care. Our main character must face death in some form, be it physical, professional or psychological. It's a short, but interesting read, and it might provide a way to unblock you, if you are stuck.

10.8 EXERCISES

1. Do you understand the basic shape of your story? Is your first crime (murder) coming at the beginning or middle of your book?

2. Fill in this simple structure with key points in your novel:

Act 1		Act 2		Act 3
'Before'	Rising Action	Mid-point	Struggle Intensifies	Resolution
*1		*2		*3

What happens at:

* 1 Inciting incident which sets your protagonist on their journey
* 2 Mid-point – something is learnt/changes and nothing will be the same
* 3 The darkest hour before the dawn

3. Write a one line description of your story. Concentrate on the essential elements. Who does it involve? What problem are they solving? What is at the heart of your story. Read it out loud to yourself. Would this summary make you want to pick up the book?

11

PLANNING FOR A SERIES

'As soon as I started thinking about publication, then this was always going to be a series.'
— Antony Johnston

It's not essential to plan a full series of books, but it's a smart thing to do, especially in the world of cozy mysteries. After all, if your first book is a success, you will want to build on this, and cozy mysteries lend themselves very happily to the development of characters and their relationships over time. In the world of publishing, editors will be looking for series potential when they consider your cozy mystery submission. It is worth thinking about this now so that you don't limit your idea's potential.

11.1 THINK AHEAD

I tend to think in threes, so have ideas for three separate books in a sequence and then an overarching story or set of threads which can be wrapped up in the third one. For me, this isn't much more than a one-liner about the longer-term arc and some half-formed thoughts in my head, but I tend to keep my ideas for a series in a file, with additional files for each proposed book, and add to these as thoughts occur.

To sustain a series, you need to combine one or more long-term story arcs, which will run over the whole series, with the shorter-term stories which will be successfully resolved in each book. Each book in the series needs to be able to stand on its own feet in providing a satisfying reading experience, as we have discussed before. The only loose ends you should leave will relate to your longer-running arcs, and while you want your readers to be desperate to pick up the next book in the series, make sure that each book creates a sense of justice served and order restored.

Your long-term story arcs could relate to an unsolved crime, perhaps something from one of your characters' pasts, or could relate to life events or relationships with your main characters, for example, whether two of your readers' favourites will get together romantically or not. In some fiction series the overarching thread would tend to involve a powerful conflict – the battle between good and evil. In cozy mysteries, these threads play more to the heart of why people read these books in terms of plot and character, with the emphasis on taking your readers on a journey with characters that they care about.

One thing to think about is whether or not your characters will age. Cozy mystery readers are well disposed to suspend disbelief and keeping your cozy world fairly timeless isn't a bad idea. On the other hand, if you want to see character development which will really engage your readers' emotions, it's probably wise to advance your series in a timely fashion and to keep a record of what happened when. This will only really create challenges if your characters are very young (and so the normal changes of growing up cannot be ignored) or very old, but people are living to a ripe old age these days.

11.2 SERIES BIBLE

An important factor in series is consistency. Each book will bring a new crime to solve and some satisfying character development, but this needs to take place within the reassurance of a familiar world for the reader. I introduced the idea of a series bible in chapter nine. Let's have a look at this in a little more detail.

A series bible is really any form of record keeping which allows you to keep track of key facts and features in your book. Typically, it would be a file or set of files listing characters, plots, key events, and so on. There are numerous ways of doing this, which include:

- Spreadsheet with different tabs for characters, places, major events/crimes
- Word file or series of files
- Physical record cards for each character
- Scrapbook or dedicated notebook

If you filled in character questionnaires for your key characters in chapter 9, you could use these as the basis for your series bible.

I have come very late to this and collated various notes into one simple Word file. I wish I had done this right from the beginning. Trust me, future you will thank present you if you start this now and update it as you go along.

11.3 EXERCISES

1. If you are intending to write a series, spend some time now jotting down ideas for one or more longer-running story threads. What will keep your reader engaged and desperate to pick up the next book from you?

2. Start a series bible! Now is the time to start record-keeping – recording key facts about your book which will ensure consistency through a series. Whether you open a new Word file, a spreadsheet, a card index or even a good old-fashioned notebook, do it today! You won't regret it.

12
SETTING

'If you're going to make setting a feature of your novel you have to make it a living, breathing character in itself.'
— Trevor Wood

With the rise of the popularity of cozy mysteries, it can feel like every possible setting already features in an existing book. Don't worry about this too much. You will bring your own experience and perspective to your writing. No-one else sees the world through your eyes.

The most successful contemporary cozy mystery series in the UK (and elsewhere) is, of course, Richard Osman's Thursday Murder Club series, set in a retirement village in the south of England. This hasn't stopped Steph Broadribb's Retired Detectives Series, set in a retirement complex in Florida, from selling extremely well. Each author brings their own take on the set up, and both series work on their own terms and have a very different feel.

Think of the number of novels set in a country village – Agatha Christie's Miss Marple, M.C. Beaton's Agatha Raisin, and so on. You would imagine that this might limit the scope for contemporary stories, but no! The desire within readers for books in rural and semi-rural England is as strong as ever. This probably taps into a collective sense of nostalgia for an idealised version of life as it used to be (when in fact the reality may have been a lot more complicated and less picturesque). Contemporary writers can take advantage of this nostalgia, while also reflecting some of the realities of rural life today.

Certain types of mystery, harking back to the classic Golden Age mysteries, involve a closed setting, in which a small number of people are isolated. When a murder occurs, and with the police cut off by inclement weather or geography, an amateur detective must step forward. There are a number of possibilities here, for example, a country house, an island, or a ship.

Urban settings are less common than rural ones in cozy mysteries, but if you define your community anything is possible. Cozy mysteries function very well in a 'community within a community' – you just need to create pockets of the world that your reader will be happy to spend time in. Derek Farrell's Danny Bird Mysteries focus on a pub in London. In choosing a supermarket in a small English town for my Supermarket Mysteries I picked a setting where 'all human life is here'. Pretty much everyone uses a supermarket at one time or another, and so I could see that my detectives would have a ready stream of potential criminals, victims and witnesses! A small town has more comings and goings than a village, while still retaining the community feel that is important in these books. The town of Kingsleigh is a figment of my imagination but is based on Keynsham, a town between Bristol and Bath in the South-West of England, where I worked for 10 years. Sharna Jackson's cozy mystery books for children/teens (High Rise Mystery and Mic Drop) are set on an inner city council estate in London.

Again, think about series potential for your setting, ways to keep things fresh or move your detectives to pastures new. There's a running joke about how many bodies pile up in one tiny village in TV's Midsomer Murders. On the whole, cozy mystery readers are willing to suspend disbelief and will forgive a growing body count in unlikely crime hotspots, but you might want to think about how you would sustain multiple books in the setting you choose.

One example is the very successful Her Majesty Investigates series by S.J. Bennett, in which the author imagines Queen Elizabeth II as an amateur detective. The books are set in different locations – Buckingham Palace, Windsor Castle, Sandringham. To ring the changes further, Bennett also visits different eras in the late Queen's life. It's a very smart, very successful idea.

12.1 CONTEMPORARY OR HISTORICAL?

Setting your mystery in the past obviously involves research into that period, which is something that many writers absolutely love. In fact, some get stuck down all sorts of research rabbit holes, so it might be a good idea to list aspects of your chosen era that you need to explore and set yourself a time frame for this phase. Be careful not to wear your research too openly on your sleeve – include just enough detail to be convincing but don't include anything 'just because you can'. The story is the thing and however much preparation work you have done, nothing should get in the way of the flow and pacing of your tale.

There is a very nice sub-genre of cozy mysteries which involves the reimagining of historical figures as amateur detectives. In Bella Ellis's Bronte Mysteries, the three Bronte sisters (and their brother) take up 'detectoring' to investigate mysteries in and around Haworth in Yorkshire in the 1840s. Other series feature Jane Austen, Charles Dickens, Oscar Wilde and Agatha Christie herself. There is a lot of fun to be had with these novels, and it's an excellent way of combining a personal interest with your own crime-writing. As Jessica Bull, author of the Miss Austen Investigates, told me in a chat on X/Twitter, 'I think a lot of historical writers like myself write the novels in order to justify doing the research!'

There will, of course, be plenty of other fans of real characters who will be eager to read these, but also may pick up on historical inaccuracies or question your interpretation of characters or events and so you will need to be confident of your take on things or be robust in your approach to fictional-isation.

12.2 EXERCISES

1. How well do you know your setting? If real, can you visit there, walk around and take some photos? Can you use Google maps or similar to research it? If imaginary, do you have a strong image of it? Would gathering some images together or drawing a map help?

2. How crucial is your setting to the crime that takes place? How might the setting itself influence the crime?

3. Imagine standing in one of the locations for your book. Spend five minutes really picturing yourself there and then write some headings at the side of your paper.

- I can see:
- I can hear:
- I can feel/taste/smell:
- What time is it?
- What season is it?
- What's the weather doing?
- Who's there?

4. If you are intending to write a historical crime story, list the topics you need to research and possible sources of information. Set yourself a time limit for this stage of your work. Remember, the story is the thing – you can always go back later and research the details that you need when you have the basic story down.

13

THEME

'To produce a mighty book, you must choose a mighty theme.'
— Herman Melville

There are two ways of looking at theme within cozy mysteries

- Theme relating to categories on Amazon, etc. e.g. animal, food, hobbies.
- An overarching theme for your story. What is this book about?

13.1 COZY MYSTERIES – CATEGORIES IN THE MARKET

While we want to write the books we love, it is also smart to keep an eye on the market. In setting out to write a cozy mystery, we are clearly aiming for one well-defined section within the crime-writing genre, and it doesn't hurt to understand how these books are currently categorised and sold via Amazon, and what sells well. Amazon is important because it is a huge player in the market. For example, its share of the ebook market in the UK is estimated by the Bookseller's Association to be around 90%.

Unless you are an established and well-loved celebrity branching into cozy mystery writing (in which case, welcome and would you like to endorse the next book in my cozy mystery series?), landing your book within a clearly defined marketing category will help Amazon to sell it and readers to find it.

On Amazon.co.uk there are three sub-categories under Cozy Mysteries:

- Cozy Animal Mysteries
- Cozy Crafts and Hobbies Mysteries
- Cozy Culinary Mysteries

I don't know the inner workings of Amazon, but it seems to me that these are following the US market, and I wonder whether this will persist or whether categories more relevant to the UK market might emerge, as there are now all sorts of witchy cozy mysteries, plus mysteries combining crime and romance. Given that this is the current status quo, though, you might want to see how your novel could fit into one of these. A bestseller flag is a bestseller flag.

To research this yourself, spend a happy hour on Amazon exploring the different charts, and how well those topping the cozy charts are selling overall. While you are doing so, make a mental note of the covers, too. A ranking of less than 20,000 in the overall chart is selling reasonably well.

For example, on 16th October 2023, Fiona Leitch's 'The Cornish Wedding Murder,' the first in her Nosey Parker series, was No. 1 in the Cozy Crafts and Hobbies Mystery, and the Cozy Culinary Mystery categories on Amazon.co.uk. It was also No. 87 in the overall Kindle chart, a position most of us would be very happy to achieve! This is for a book first published in 2021, with five others already out and a sixth to come in 2024. More evidence that a successful series is the gift that keeps on giving!

13.2 OVERARCHING PLOT AND UNDERLYING THEME – WHAT IS YOUR BOOK ABOUT?

This is another reminder to always bear in mind what lies at the very core of your book. In Chapter 10, we attempted to write a one sentence summary of our book. If you don't have this off pat, then take a little more time to work on it now. Revisit it at various stages of your novel-writing process – it's fine to keep revising it so that it truly reflects the book you have written.

There may also be an underlying theme, perhaps an emotional one which you (and your readers) will feel deeply and appreciate – yes, it's a crime story but the real theme may be that friendship matters, or that you should hold your dear ones close or whatever. Perhaps theme is the wrong word here, but you may read over your first draft and realise, 'Oh, it's a book about betrayal.' Sometimes these revelations can be as much of a surprise to you as a writer and they are to the reader (or maybe the reader is ahead of you).

When I wrote my first published book, a YA thriller, 'Numbers,' about a girl who can see death dates in people's eyes, I read through the first draft, thinking I'd written a paranormal thriller and realised that I'd written a love story, which came as a bit of a surprise. In fact, it's both, which is fine. (A bit more than fine, to be honest – given its sales figures and multi-country appeal.)

As a writer, it is interesting to see what themes or undercurrents recur in your work – they are often the things that really matter to you. You might not set out to use writing as therapy, but you will certainly learn things about yourself along the way.

13.3 EXERCISES

1. Have you considered where your book might fit within the genre? Search the Amazon book charts to see which categories are currently selling well and see if your book would fit any of these categories. Is there a way to tweak your plot or characters so that your book would fit more squarely into an Amazon category?

. . .

2. What is your book about? Print or write
   out the one-liner you wrote in Chapter 10.
   Does it still sum up your book? Could you
   revise it to give it more of a hook?

14
FINDING YOUR VOICE

'To capture her tone, I immersed myself in her letters to her sister and her juvenilia – in which she is more candid. It was this Austen I wanted to capture, the effervescent young woman...'
— Jessica Bull

Finding your voice, or at least the right voice for each book, is crucial. The voice sets the all-pervading style and feel of the book and influences the way the reader perceives the story. What makes up the voice is quite difficult to define, but includes point of view, tense, tone, attitude, and emotion.

14.1 POINT OF VIEW

There are three conventional points of view; first person, second person and third person.

First person is written from one character's viewpoint and the action is seen through their eyes and with their knowledge, using the pronoun 'I.' It is useful in building tension and suspense, as we live the story at the same time as our protagonist, and is most commonly found in thrillers, particularly psychological and domestic thrillers.

Second person is written using the pronoun you and involves the narrator directly addressing someone (which could include the reader, effectively breaking the fourth wall dividing the book from its audience). It's a tricky, rarely used point of view, although one shining example is The Appeal by Janice Hallett, which is told using emails, texts and messages to brilliant effect.

Third person is written using the pronouns he, she and they. It allows the story to follow multiple characters and their narrative arcs. There are different forms of third person, ranging from all knowing/seeing to focusing close in on one character, so I'll break it down a little (Source: Master-class.com):

- Third-person Omniscient – the narrator knows everything about the story and its characters, including what they are thinking and feeling and may comment on the action as it unfolds (think Jane Austen's Pride and Prejudice).
- Third-person Limited, also known as close third – the narrator sticks closely to one character at a time, but stays in third using he, she or they. The viewpoint can switch between characters but, for the reader's sake, this needs to be done carefully to avoid 'head-hopping' so is best done at a natural break like a new chapter or the beginning of a major scene. When choosing which character to follow, you need to consider who is the main actor in the scene, who has the most at stake or biggest role to play.
- Third-person Objective – the narrator is a neutral observer, who does not have insight into the characters' thoughts or feelings.

This gives the reader the feeling of being a witness or eavesdropper.

In a quick study of the twenty top selling cozy mysteries on Amazon.co.uk I found that eighteen were written in third person point of view, with two written in first person. This confirmed my suspicion that for cozy mysteries, third person, usually close third, is the voice that most writers in the genre gravitate towards. It allows you to get inside your character's heads to some degree, but without the limitation that first person point of view can impose, that of only knowing what that character knows or only following the action in one location. In my Supermarket Mysteries, I tend to write in close third, focusing on my main protagonist, Bea, but occasionally swapping to follow Ant when he is pursuing the investigation elsewhere.

As Julia Chapman, author of the Dales Detectives series, said in an interview with me, 'The added difficulty of getting those voices right is offset by the added flexibility you get in terms of setting, perspective, and the way you can move the plot around.'

14.2 TENSE

Another choice that faces you is the tense you choose. Present tense describes the action as it happens as in, 'He sees the murderer,' or 'She finds a crucial clue.' Past tense describes what has already happened, so, 'He saw the murderer,' or 'She found a crucial clue.'

I had assumed that cozy mysteries would mostly be told in the past tense, and, again, this is true but not overwhelmingly so. Fourteen of the top twenty cozy mysteries that I studied were past tense, while six were present tense. This picture might be a little skewed by four of the present tense books being the Thursday Murder Club series, but it is worth considering the success of these books. Obviously, being written by a well-loved celebrity gave the books an initial boost, but I know that readers adore them in their own right, and a large part of it, I believe, is the voice. Being third-person present tense is a point of difference with many other books in this genre and gives them a personality of their own. It seems to be to be another smart choice by Richard Osman.

For most writers, using past tense is the natural choice for these stories. While you can - and should - build tension, surprising readers with plot twists and reveals, past tense tends to give a less visceral reading experience. There is a little distance between the reader and the action. The reader also knows that the drama is already over and can expect everything to be resolved by the end of the story.

14.3 TONE AND LANGUAGE

Cozy mysteries aim to provide agreeable entertainment for their readers. They are mostly written in a straightforward, neutral style, often with the tone being set by close third point of view which gives the reader a taste of their main character's (or characters') likeable, engaging or amusing view of proceedings. Mysteries with a historical setting may be written with language more fitting to that period, either harking back to the comic tones of PG Woodhouse or to darker prose, for example, the Bronte Mysteries.

It is worth experimenting with your prose until you hit on a balance that works for you. The right tone can be a rather nebulous thing to achieve, and it may be a matter of the smallest of tweaks to the vocabulary used. Much of this will relate back to the character work you have already done. When you truly know and understand your main characters you will find that their voice starts coming through in your writing.

14.4 EXERCISES

1. If you are struggling to choose the point of view for your story, write a scene or part of a scene in first person and then third person. Does it make you see the scene differently? Does one style come more naturally to you? How does the point of view affect how the story comes across?

2. If you are struggling to choose the right tense for your story, write a scene or part of a scene in present tense and then past tense. How does it make you feel about the story? Will one or the other limit the way your story unfolds? Which feels more natural to you as a storyteller?

3. If you are struggling with voice or tone, go back to your character profiles. Is there more work you can do here to get to know your characters, understand their view of the world and their 'take' on things? Try and list five adjectives they would use about themselves. Then list five that their best friend or close family member would use about them. Build up a more rounded picture and see if that helps.

Appendix 1

Analysis of Top Twenty Cozy Mystery books on Amazon.co.uk, POV and Tense, 18/10/23, by Rachel Ward.

	Present Tense	Past Tense
1st Person POV	0	2
3rd Person POV	6	12

15

BRINGING THE WARMTH

"No act of kindness, no matter how small, is ever wasted."
— Aesop

While cozy mysteries include murder and intrigue, they should not give your readers nightmares. As we have discussed, all but the mildest violence takes place off screen in these books but the absence of something isn't what really brings the warmth to a cozy mystery. What does is the way the stories are infused with elements that reassure readers and balance any darkness with light – humour, kindness, relationships, even food.

15.1 HUMOUR

In everyday life, we use humour as a form of currency in our transactions with other people. Often it's a way to try and make people like you. Sometimes we use humour to diffuse tension or break the ice. Think of the way you and your friends and family use humour and then see how you might apply that to your characters. What makes you smile? Word play? A little light bitching about someone? Cynicism? Do you have in-jokes or running jokes with family members or friends?

Cozy mysteries tend to have a lightness of touch running through them, which can be a question of tone and voice, as we found out in the previous chapter. For example, the narrator's voice in The Thursday Murder Club series describes what the characters feel about things (in close third person) with more than a hint of Osman's own good-natured, wisecracking tone. There's no need to copy this - as you write, you will bring your own tone and sense of humour to your book.

Flashes of humour lighten the mood. Depending on the overall feel of your book and where it sits on the cozy scale, humour can be used liberally or sparingly, but a cozy mystery without any humour at all won't work.

15.2 DIALOGUE

Writing humour isn't easy. In these books, the humour tends not to be jokes, but the sort of banter and observations that people have every day, which brings us to the role of dialogue. The way your characters speak with each other reveals so much about them – how they view themselves and their role in the world, how they view other people, their personality, communication style, and the state of their relationship with the other person.

I often find that I start a scene with the dialogue, a bit like a screenplay, and then go back to add in reactions and descriptions. Remember to make it clear to your reader who is speaking, but not to pepper your text with 'he said, she said.' Use these identifiers sparingly and watch out for alternatives to the humble 'said.' My handy grammar advisor in Word, the software that I use on my PC, is always suggesting other ways of saying 'said' but unless you want to indicate particularly heightened volume or emotion, keep it simple. Your dialogue should be doing the work here, showing your reader the emotional state of your characters through what they say, and too many unusual verbs or adverbs may destroy the flow.

If you find writing dialogue difficult, indulge in a bit of eavesdropping. Listen to people and how they speak to each other. Try transcribing conversations to understand how people actually use language. I love writing on trains and was hoping for a productive couple of hours on one journey from the West Country to London. Unfortunately, I was in a carriage with some very loud, rather inebriated, and frankly, posh, young men. Instead of quietly fuming or getting in a huff and trying to find a seat elsewhere, I started writing down exactly what they were saying. It was fascinating!

If you struggle with dialogue, another tip is to try reading it out loud (or to the cat or dog in your life, if they are willing to listen). You can record yourself and listen back, if you want to, but usually the actual act of speaking your text aloud will quickly enable you to identify sections, phrases or words that don't ring true or interrupt the flow. This applies to any piece of writing, but I do think that it's particularly helpful in highlighting any problems with dialogue. Give it a try!

15.3 KINDNESS

If our readers are looking for comfort in our books, then showing our characters' kindness is important. This can contribute hugely to their likeability, which as we established earlier, is a key aspect of these books. Again, as screenwriter Blake Snyder emphasises, an act of kindness can quickly indicate the sort of character that readers will want to get to know.

I love writing about the friendship between my main characters in my Supermarket Mysteries, Bea and Ant. Throughout the books, they show compassion and kindness for each other. Bea is sympathetic to Ant's struggles with housing and illiteracy. Ant provides a shoulder to cry on when Bea's love life goes wrong or she's just down in the dumps. The thing that packs an emotional punch for me in the fourth book, however, is a little scene in which Ant shows compassion for a character with whom he has a prickly relationship, Neville. When Neville is struggling with issues from his past, Ant is prepared to listen and sit with him quietly, and writing that scene brought a tear to my eye (in a good way).

15.4 RELATIONSHIPS

The way that you handle relationships within your novel will not only shape how your readers feel about this book but will make them want to read the next one and the next.

Obviously, the key relationship will be between your main protagonists, however many you have decided on. This can play out in a number of ways. In movies and TV shows, the obvious trope for a pair of police detectives is for them to hate each other when they meet, but gradually find out more about each other and learn to get along, for example, Martin Riggs (played by Mel Gibson) and Roger Murtaugh (played by Danny Glover) in the 1980s movie Lethal Weapon, or more recently Sunny Kahn and Jessica James in the series of TV detective show Unforgotten. In cozy mysteries, we can play with that pattern, too, but we also should not be afraid of portraying full-on friendships. After all, we are planning to put our protagonists through many, many adventures together (as our series goes from strength to strength).

Some cozy mysteries involve a romantic element between two of the detectives, often keeping the reader guessing whether they will eventually get together. This is a fun thing to play with over a number of books.

Think about your minor characters, too. Try to make them as rounded as you can. It will make for a richer reading experience, plus you never know if they might need to step forward into the limelight in a future book.

Of course, not all is sweetness and light in cozy mysteries. Some mysteries feature victims who are so unpleasant that the reader won't feel bad at their demise. (This applies to several of Agatha Christie's murder victims.) Our criminals are often hiding their dark side until all is revealed at the end. We can also have side characters who are a bit shady and contribute their underworld knowledge and dodgy contacts to solving the mystery. The way our detectives relate to these characters will reveal much about who they are, and we can bring humour here as well, when we need to balance out the light and dark.

15.5 FOOD

Cozy culinary mysteries are a whole sub-genre according to Amazon, but I believe we can use food to very good effect in any cozy story. Food is such a transactional thing and is often a useful shorthand way of giving readers insight into a character or relationship. There is so much that can be explored: sharing food, cooking together, being a feeder or being cooked for, paying or being paid for, comfort food, junk food, fast food or food to savour.

Orlando Murrin who wrote 'Knife Skills for Beginners', set in a cookery school, says, 'The way people cook tells you a lot about their personality.' My main characters in the Supermarket Mysteries work in the food-rich environment of a small-town food store. At the start of the series, I enjoyed contrasting the huge potential offered by Bea's workplace with the very strict rota of uninspiring fare which her mother cooks for her. In more recent books, as her mother's mental health improves, her cooking becomes more adventurous. Meanwhile, Ant and Bea's relationship is fostered over numerous trips to the local chip shop.

Whether our books feature professional chefs or

amateurs, or even if we just feature fleeting references to food, I like to think of cozy mysteries as the 'comfort food' of the crime fiction world.

15.6 EXERCISES

1. Spend ten minutes jotting down a conversation between two inanimate objects, maybe a pen and paper, or a couple of children's toys. You might surprise yourself how much you manage to show about their different personalities and their relationship in a short, light-hearted chat.

2. Spend five or ten minutes transcribing a real-life conversation – either something you overhear or a radio interview or podcast. It's interesting to record how people speak to each other, the language (formal, informal, slang, nicknames) whether they use half-formed sentences, the hesitations and gaps.

．　．　．

3. Think about the role of food in your book.
    What is the favourite food of your main
    characters? Does food bring people
    together in your stories, or are your
    characters eating on the run, or skipping
    meals?

16
BELIEVABILITY

'The difference between fiction and reality? Fiction has to make sense.'
— Tom Clancy

*M*ost cozy mysteries ask the reader to suspend disbelief, just a little bit. While 'civilians' do, of course, sometimes solve crimes in the real world and there are wonderful examples of ordinary people tracking down stolen property or helping to find missing persons, in reality it is very rare for non-police personnel to solve one murder, let alone a whole string of them!

On the whole, our readers know what they are

going to get in a cozy mystery and they are happy to go along with the concept of a crime-solving chef or checkout worker or retired spy. Other than this, though, it is important not to have gaps, plot holes or glaring errors in the story as a whole. The situations and puzzles that our characters face, and their actions, should all pass the believability test within the context we have set.

Crime readers are discerning and knowledgeable. Many readers (you may be one of them, I certainly am) devour crime fiction and become extremely well-versed in the various plotlines, character tropes and twists that are the bread and butter of crime-writing. Just because the readers of cozy mysteries are looking for 'light entertainment' doesn't mean that they will not notice or accept sloppiness in our writing. So, it is worth having a read through of your work for believability and keeping in mind the following points.

16.1 KEEP A TIMELINE

Keep a timeline for your book. You can add plot developments and times or dates as you go along, or you can write out a timeline after you have finished your first draft. Make sure that little things like days of the week and dates tally.

16.2 CONSIDER MODERN TECHNOLOGY – USE IT OR LOSE IT!

If your book is contemporary, you may need to come up with a reason why your characters can't just use their phones or laptops to Google everything, or why your detective rushes off in pursuit of someone instead of just calling their mobile or whatever. Unless you are Janice Hallett and use emails and messages as a basis for your book, modern methods of communication can sometimes make crime-solving seem a bit too easy, but there are ways around this.

As Julia Chapman, author of the Dales Detectives series, says, 'It's so frustrating when modern tech is ignored simply for the sake of the plot. But at the same time, too much can make things clumsy. A fine balance needs to be struck between the two.'

16.3 CHECK HISTORICAL DETAILS

If your book has a historical setting, check the period details. Consider the language that your characters would use. I wouldn't say your language and mode of speech have to be 100% accurate, but readers will notice modern slang and some will not like it!

For S.J. Bennett, author of the Her Majesty Investigates series, fact-checking is vitally important. When I interviewed her, she said, 'I'm always clear that this is fiction! The Queen did not, to the best of my knowledge, solve crimes. But that aside, I try to be as authentic as possible. Readers are more likely to believe her mystery-solving adventures if they take place between known events.'

16.4 FOOLS RUSH IN…

Towards the end of your book, you will want to raise the stakes and have at least one of your key characters in danger. Try to make sure that this key scene (or sequence of scenes) is credible. Why does your detective go into a dark, spooky house on their own? Why don't they wait for the police to come before confronting the person they think is responsible for murder? It may be that there is a ticking clock and so your sleuth simply cannot wait for reinforcements, or perhaps your two main characters have had an argument which leads to one of them going it alone. Make sure that your readers are swept along with the action as your book reaches its climax, rather than scratching their heads and saying, 'Hang on, I don't buy that…'

16.5 COINCIDENCES

Try not to develop a plot that relies on too many coincidences. You will probably get away with one, but more than that will stretch your readers' patience. If you find your plot is too reliant on chance, fate and coincidence, take some time to think about ways of making it more solid and satisfying.

16.5 EXERCISES

1. Sorry to nag, but if you haven't started a series bible yet, now is the time to open a new file and start one today. Include a timeline of events and key characters' names, addresses and occupations.

. . .

2. Consider how technology may help or hinder your detectives. Do you need a device to cut them off from modern communications? How can you do that seamlessly?

17

A WORD ABOUT TITLES

'What's in a name? That which we call a rose by any other name would smell as sweet.'
— William Shakespeare, Romeo and Juliet

Titles are an extremely important part of marketing your book. The right title on a well-designed cover will position your book clearly in its genre and prompt potential readers to find out more (and possibly buy). Some writers like to have a title in mind when they start their first draft. Others have working titles, which may change along the way.

If you are published traditionally, your publisher will have a view about the title, and may well change it (ideally, but not always, with your enthusiastic agreement). For me, playing with title ideas is part of the fun, but I've learned not to get too attached, in case there are changes later.

If you are one of those people who needs a good working title, have a look at similar books on the cozy mystery listings online or visit a local bookshop. What would sum up your book and give readers a clear message about what your story will offer them? Also, bear in mind that your first title will hopefully set the pattern for a series. So, ideally you want to come up with something – a particular number of words, a format or a pun – that matches your current book but also sets the tone for a series and offers the potential to ring the changes over multiple follow ups.

17.1 EXERCISE

1. Just for fun, have a quick ideas session on potential titles. Jot down ten title ideas – don't think too much about it, write the ideas down as they come to you. Have a look back. Do any of them stand out? Do they sum up your book or at least give the reader a good idea what to expect?

. . .

2. Have a look through the Cozy Mystery charts on Amazon (or any other online retailer). Is there a common theme with titles? Can you come up with a title for your book which would sit happily among the books in the current chart?

18

WRITE YOUR FIRST DRAFT – HOW TO DEVELOP GOOD WRITING HABITS

'You can always edit a bad page. You can't edit a blank page.'
— Jodi Picoult

Well, we're finally here. You've got your characters, you've plotted things out to one extent or another, you have an idea of your theme and what your book is actually about, and now it's time to write your first draft.

Remember, a first draft is rarely a thing of beauty. Whether you have planned things in detail or not, it might help to think of this as a discovery draft. If you more robustly inclined, call it a vomit draft. This is the stage when you get all those thoughts and ideas

102

onto the screen or page. This is when you tell yourself the story.

18.1 FORM A WRITING HABIT

In terms of actually getting a draft written, it is a question of finding what works for you. The usual advice is write every day and get into a routine. A little progress five or seven days a week adds up really quickly. I wrote my first book in daily sessions of 45 minutes, early in the morning, before everyone else woke up and before I went to work at my day job. Working like this, I completed a first draft in six months.

However, for some people a daily practice just isn't possible. You may be juggling all sorts of commitments – paid work, family stuff, caring responsibilities, health conditions – which mean that you can only write on one or two days a week, or just one morning, or a few days a month. Any writing time is valuable, and you will work out what fits with your lifestyle.

I find that writing with others is really effective and I nearly always attend one of the London Writers' Salon's Writers' Hours. These are Zoom sessions which take place four times a day on weekdays, with one session on a Saturday morning (UK time). At The Writers' Hour (writershour.com) you can sign up for free, or there are membership options with additional benefits. There is something about the accountability and fellowship of writing silently with people from across the globe that really helps me to focus, and it may work for you. You could have a similar arrangement with your own writing buddies as well, of course – agreeing to meet online and write for a set time, and maybe chat afterwards and get a bit of peer support.

18.2 SET A TIMER

If you find your concentration wavering, try setting a timer and commit to write for twenty minutes or even ten. The chances are that you will hit your stride and naturally continue after this time. Or you can follow the Pomodoro method which is to set a timer and write for twenty-five minutes, then take a five-minute break away from your screen, then back for another twenty-five and so on.

18.3 SET WORD TARGETS

Setting word targets can help, too. When I am writing a first draft, I aim for a thousand words a day, which is usually achievable for me. I must stress that these are not perfect words. I try to write fairly cleanly, but at this stage getting it down is more important than getting it right. At this pace, I can have a first draft done in two or three months. From my experience, it is better to set a low target and over-achieve (patting yourself on the back as you do so) than to have one that is unrealistically high and sets you up to fail.

18.4 FIND A PLACE TO WRITE

If you are lucky, you might have a home office or writing shed in which to work. Many of us make do with a PC in the corner of a room, or a laptop on the kitchen table. Find what works for you. If working at home is too distracting – the washing machine needs feeding, the floors have muddy footprints, the dog wants you to play ball – try taking your laptop to a café or local library. I usually work at home, but if I'm having difficulty focusing, I spend an hour or so at the library, where I can get a surprising amount of work done. Sometimes switching things up or breaking out of a rut is the key to progress. This quote from Dani Shapiro sums it up.

'And so we need a sense of structure around us. These four walls. This cup. The wheels of the train beneath us. This borrowed room. The weight of this particular pen. Whatever it is that makes us feel secure in our physical space allows us to make the leap, hoping that the page will catch us. Writing, after all is an act of faith. We must believe, without the slightest evidence that believing will get us anywhere."

18.5 TAKE REGULAR BREAKS

More isn't always better in terms of screen time. If you find yourself sitting at your desk for hours on end and the words aren't flowing, it's definitely a sign to take a break. Self-care is important, so please remember to keep hydrated, and to stretch to preserve the health of your back, neck and arm muscles. There are plenty of videos online aimed at computer users like us, but I would recommend yoga stretches and find that Yoga with Adriene has a range of videos that help to keep me mobile.

18.6 HOW LONG SHOULD MY FIRST DRAFT BE?

At this stage, I wouldn't worry too much about how long your draft is. Tell yourself the story and see what you've got at the end. There isn't one ideal word count for a cozy mystery, as the range varies according to the model of publishing that you are aiming for. As a broad guideline, traditional publishers may look for up to 90 thousand words (longer if you are a celebrity or other mega-seller), digital-first publishers will accept shorter novels 60-70 thousand and for self-publishing, 50 thousand plus is fine.

18.7 EXERCISES

1. Think about your schedule and commitments – when can you find time to write? Add writing slots to your diary and turn them from intentions to commitments.

2. If one way of writing is not working for
   you, try something else! Go to the library
   or a café, try a group writing session on
   Zoom (London Writers' Salon), set a timer,
   take a break. Change things up and find
   what works for you.

19

WHAT TO DO WHEN YOU GET STUCK

'Consider this mindset, never in a hurry, never worried, never desperate, never stopping short... There's no need to sweat this or feel rushed. You're in this for the long haul... temporary setbacks aren't discouraging. They are just bumps along a long road that you intend to travel all the way down.'

— Ryan Holiday, The Obstacle is the Way

Even if you find a time of day and a routine that fits your style of working, it is almost inevitable that you will get stuck at some point and may encounter one of the following:

- You find yourself lacking energy and focus.

- You don't know what comes next.
- You lose confidence in your story and your
  ability to write it.

The first thing is – don't panic. If writing was easy, everyone would do it! We may all 'have a book in us', but very few of us do the research, plan ahead, set ourselves up to succeed and then show the grit and persistence needed to actually complete a first draft. You have started on this road and you're now facing a bit of a bump. You can and will get over it. You *will* find your own way forward, and there are lots of tips and tricks to help you negotiate a sticky patch and keep making progress. Here are some of the things that I have found useful:

- **Have a break**! Walk, swim, have a bath,
  bake a cake or cook something healthy,
  draw, paint, go to an exhibition. A change is
  as good as a rest. Sitting in the same
  position and staring at a screen is fine if the
  words are flowing, but if you've come to a
  standstill, you need a physical change of
  scene and you need to give your brain a
  break.

- **Rest**! Getting up early or staying up late to write can take its toll. Michael Mosley, the health writer, espoused the benefits of a short nap, which he described as 'not a lazy snooze, it's a brain booster! Napping can help your heart, improve your mood and enhance your memory… and may even boost your creativity.' In my experience, an afternoon nap will often result in a refreshed brain that is ready for another writing session.

- **Set your brain to solve the task overnight**. The human brain is a wonderful thing. Sometimes when I am stuck on a plot point or not quite knowing 'what comes next' I deliberately think about it before I go to sleep. When I sit down to write the next morning, the answer can be there (not always, but it's worth a try). My brain has been quietly mulling things over while I'm asleep and produced the solution.

- **Jump ahead and write the end.** If you have the end in mind, it can be extremely helpful to write it down and then work out what steps you need in order to join the gap between your earlier chapters and the end. It doesn't matter if you need to change things when you finally get there – this version will have served its purpose.

- **Jump ahead and write any scene.** Sometimes particular scenes or passages of dialogue are extremely vivid to you. Write them down in a 'Spare' file. This may help you to free up your thinking, possibly by working out how you can reach these key scenes. If your saved scenes slot in as they are, so much the better. If they need modifying, that's fine too.

- **Go back to your plan**, if you made one. It might be that you have already thought through the next step and written it down! Just revisiting the structure that you set out initially could be enough to prompt you now. Maybe you have veered from your plan and need to revise it to reflect how the story is actually panning out. There's no harm in that. Spend a happy hour with some sticky notes or the cork board on Scrivener, which is a word processing and outlining program specifically designed for writers, or whatever tool you like using and play with ideas and 'what ifs.'

- **Draw up a plan for the next section**. If your overarching plan isn't particularly detailed, maybe now is the time to look ahead to the next section and try and scope out the stages/chapters/scenes that you need. How can the next section support the 3 or 5 act structure? Is your mid-section missing its crucial mid-point? How can each chapter in the next section contribute to the progress of your story? A little bit of fine-grained thinking at this point may help you move forward.

- **Use flip chart paper to make notes**. It may seem like a flippant suggestion (pun intended, my apologies) but the different feeling of stepping away from your screen and 'thinking big' can be enough to kickstart your brain and unlock blockages. I have got a pad of flip chart paper that sticks to the wall, like giant post-it note. It's very liberating to start at the top of a huge blank sheet and fill it with branching 'what if' trains of thought.

- **Do some writing exercises**. It may be that your brain is stuck in a rut. Try some short writing exercises to free your thinking. There are plenty of free ones online – so pick a writing prompt or a dialogue exercise or anything that will take you out of your lane for a little while.

- **Freewriting/journalling/morning pages**. Perhaps your brain is full of a hundred and one things alongside your novel. One way to clear the mental decks is to write down your thoughts at the start of the day. Julia Cameron, author of 'The Artist's Way: A Spiritual Path to Higher Creativity' suggests developing a daily practice she calls 'Morning Pages.' This is 'three pages of longhand, stream of consciousness writing done first thing in the morning. There is no wrong way to do Morning Pages – they are not high art. They are not even 'writing.' They are about anything and everything that crosses your mind – and they are for your eyes only.' Many people find that having committed these thoughts to paper, they are then ready for the day's work.

- **Don't agonise about not meeting your word count target**. While ideally we would all like to have the perfect writing routine, complete our target word count every day, and finish a first draft in weeks rather than months (or years), life isn't usually like that. Thinking, making notes, playing with ideas, and taking a goddamn break are all part of writing. Sometimes life just gets in the way and you have to give priority to other things. You've got this far, though. If you cannot write for a while, for whatever reason, your story, your characters, the joy you find in writing about them, will wait for you. You can pick up where you left off, and maybe you will appreciate the magic of writing just a little bit more.

- **Boost your confidence – help yourself to a little pep talk!** If you are doubting yourself and asking 'Why me? Why did I ever think I can do this?' switch the question around. 'Why not me?' The difference between you and thousands of potential writers who fall by the wayside is persistence.

- In opening this book and reading this far, you've already shown a commitment to getting your draft written. And now, day by day, writing session by writing session, you can do it. You have the ideas. You've done your prep. You have the tools to do it. It's all a question of putting in the work. Think how amazing it will feel to finish this draft! And you *can* do it. Writers aren't magical beings, imbued with mystical powers (well, most of us aren't anyway). We are people with ideas, people who love stories and people who are prepared to put in the time and the work to commit words – thousands of words - to the page. *You are a writer. You can do this. Believe in yourself. I believe in you.*

(Full disclosure, this is the first non-fiction book I've written and so the pep talk is directed at me as much as you.)

19.1 EXERCISES

1. If you can't write at all, have a break or rest. Give yourself permission to do something else entirely. Try fresh air and/or exercise or do something to refresh your creative well – go to a movie or an exhibition, read something outside your genre, watch TV!

2. If you do have the headspace to write, but don't know what happens next in your novel, try revisiting your plan, jumping ahead or writing notes on a huge piece of paper.

3. If you are doubting yourself and your abilities to do this, congratulations, you're a writer! Self-doubt definitely comes with the territory. Try some simple affirmations. Talk to yourself as you would talk to a good friend. If they were beset by worries, what

would you say to them to reassure them
and spur them on?

20

YOU'VE WRITTEN A FIRST DRAFT, WHAT NEXT?

'Books aren't written, they're rewritten. Including your own. It is one of the hardest things to accept, especially after the seventh rewrite hasn't quite done it...'
— Michael Crichton

When you've finished your first draft, it's fine to take a little time to pat yourself on the back. So many people have an idea (a surefire, commercial hit, of course, as they will no doubt tell you when they hear that you are a writer) but don't commit it to paper or the screen. Many others will start to write a novel but won't complete it. Getting to the end of a first draft is an accomplishment in itself and you should feel really proud.

It's important to celebrate the good moments in a writing life, so do mark this milestone! Raise a glass to yourself, have a chocolate biscuit with your tea, do a little victory dance, go out for a meal, high five the dog. You did it!

The best advice now is to take a break from your document or manuscript. Put it aside for a little while. If you can't bear not to write, work on something else. Maybe you had an idea that was niggling away at you while you were writing this book. Hopefully, you wrote it down and filed it away. Now's the time to revisit it, if you want to. Or do something completely different and give your weary brain a rest.

20.1 WRITING IS REWRITING

'I have spreadsheets and all sorts these days, but it's ultimately this; don't worry in draft 1, but in draft 2, read it like a reader. What do you need to know and when? Be strict with yourself!'
— S.J. Bennett

Ideally, you would leave your manuscript alone for at least a week - maybe a fortnight or even longer – so that you come back to it with fresh eyes. You can read though it on screen, of course. Some writers prefer to print the whole thing out so they can make editorial notes on the page. You can also send a Word file to a Kindle (I'm not sure if this works for other e-readers). Just send an email to your Kindle address, (which is the first part of your Amazon ID/email address with @kindle.com) and attach your file. You will usually then receive an email asking you to verify the document. Once verified your document is delivered instantly. Alternatively, you can go directly to amazon.com/sendtokindle and upload a file directly. (It's a rather delicious feeling to read your book on a Kindle for the first time – you can savour how it will be when it is out in the world and other people are reading it just like this.)

Read it through and make 'broad brush' notes on bigger issues to fix (or little ones if they are really bugging you).

Now, revisit your log line or one line pitch. On reading your first draft, what is your book about? Books change and evolve as we write them. It's normal to develop insight about our stories as they unfold. How has that changed the essence of your book? I know I keep banging on about it, but the one-liner is the gateway to agents, publishers, foreign publishers, TV and film executives.

When it comes to editing, don't try to do everything at once. Tackle one thing at a time. I'd suggest starting with the broadest brush first and working towards the finer details on each edit.

20.2 STRUCTURE, PACING, PLOT ARCS (THIS COULD BE MORE THAN ONE EDIT)

Does your story flow and 'feel' right? Did anything jar or leave you hanging when you read it? Do you hook your reader in at the beginning? Were there sections in the middle that even you were tempted to skip?

If you wrote a plan before starting your novel, now is the time to revisit this. It's normal to diverge from a plan during the writing process, as new ideas occur to you and characters start to come to life. It's worth reviewing how this has affected the shape of your story. Does it still hit significant marks at the right point, for example, the inciting incident, the midpoint, the crisis? You can revise the plan, if you like, or just read it through and make some notes on areas that need fixing.

If you didn't plan, looking at your novel in terms

of classic story structure might help, so this could be the time to revisit chapter 10.

For example, I had got nearly two thirds of the way through the fifth book in my cozy mystery series when I had the nagging feeling that it wasn't working. I read it through, bearing in mind basic story structure, and realised that I had gone wrong at the start. My set up and the inciting incident (discovery of the first body) had not been handled well and didn't launch my characters into their investigation in a sufficiently compelling way. It needed a complete rewrite, which was irksome at the time, but resulted in a much better draft.

In terms of pacing, a cozy mystery doesn't need to rattle along at breakneck speed, but it *is* a mystery, and so it needs to maintain a certain momentum in order to keep the reader interested. Pay attention to how you end each chapter. If you can't find a cliffhanger for each chapter end (which would be a little exhausting in a cozy mystery), at least try and raise a question in the reader's mind so that they want to start the next one.

The middle section is the one where the pace is most likely to slacken off and your plot may start meandering. Believe me, I have spent plenty of time wrestling with a 'soggy middle'. If this has happened to you, revisit your plan. Or go to the middle of the book, see if you have a pivotal moment and work both ways from that. What needs to lead up to it? What will happen as a consequence? Have a good look at the spine of your story – the main crime or mystery. If you are confident that you have handled that well, perhaps your story is missing a sub-plot to divert and entertain your reader. Many crime books have at least two plot threads running through them. In a cozy mystery, your sub-plot doesn't necessarily have to be about crime – it could focus on another problem or issue in your main character's life and it has potential to bring more human interest, warmth and humour into your book.

Cozy mysteries may sit at the fuzzy end of the crime scale, but they *are* crime books, and so you will need to observe the conventions of general crime-writing. You need a sufficient number of suspects to keep your reader guessing, and enough red herrings to provide intrigue and entertainment. Cozy mystery readers love solving a puzzle, and at this stage, you need to check that your mystery element works.

This stage of editing is not easy! Orlando Murrin says, 'With a crime book where it's so intricately plotted, the redrafting is particularly complicated.' Each change affects the plot throughout the rest of the book. As well as dealing with the implications of this, cozy mystery writers also have to keep an eye on how 'delicate humour gets shaken up, too.'

20.3 CHARACTER DEVELOPMENT

I would suggest having one whole edit focusing on how your characters develop through the book. Where do they start? What do they learn? In what state does the book leave them? Certainly, look at this for your protagonists, but it may also be worth doing for your key side characters. As well as focusing on your characters' 'journey' in this book, think about the potential for character development across your series. Have you sown the seeds for future storylines or blocked off any potentially useful developments?

20.4 CONSISTENCY, SPELLING, PUNCTUATION

Once you are happy with your plot and characters, do an in-depth sweep for consistency, punctuation and spelling. Fix as many little things as you can. Trust me, you may pick up a lot at this stage, but there will be more. This first sweep is just the beginning!

Editing may take as long as writing the first draft, or longer. It can be frustrating, but I urge you with every fibre of my being, not to send your book anywhere (agent, publisher) or publish it yourself until you are satisfied that it is the best it can be. Before you send it to anyone in publishing, it's time to be brave and share it with someone else.

As Steph Carey, Senior Commissioning Editor at Bonnier says, 'We're never looking for a print-ready book, but as a general rule I'd say it's worth putting your best foot forward when submitting. So, the MS should ideally be free from any silly obvious mistakes. Use Spellcheck and try to read things through as you write – this will really help. And if you can get a beta-reader, even better.'

20.5 A SECOND PAIR OF EYES

By the time you have read your manuscript a few times, it is difficult to see the wood for the trees. I know how hard it is to share your work, but at this stage you really need someone to bring a fresh perspective to your writing – a beta reader. This needs to be someone who will give honest feedback, not tell you what they think you want to hear. It could be a family member – my husband is excellent at giving feedback on my work and can point out where things aren't working in a kind way. I think it's quite unusual in a loved one, and only you can judge whether it is likely to work in your case. Non-writer friends may also be good readers, but, again, make sure they are familiar with your genre and aren't afraid to be honest with you. I would recommend finding another writer to be your beta reader. You can read each other's work in a spirit of writerly support and comradeship! You can have more than one beta reader – it certainly reinforces the message if several people pick up on the same thing in a book but can be confusing if the feedback is mixed or contradictory.

You can pay for editorial input. There are plenty of agencies and freelance editors and mentors, which you can find online or via word-of-mouth recommendations. If you are intending to self-publish, paying for a thorough edit is highly recommended.

You may also want to get the opinion of someone with particular experience or expertise in an area. This is more common in other genres (for example, seeking the advice of a former police officer if you are writing a police procedural), but there may be issues around marginalised people that you want to get right, in which case seek out a sensitivity reader and be prepared to pay the going rate for their opinion.

20.6 HOW TO REACT TO FEEDBACK

Having asked for feedback – from a friend or family member or another writer – you have to deal with it when it comes. This is one of the hardest lessons I have learned over the years. At the start of my writing career, I used to take editorial advice very badly. It felt like a personal attack! There was sulking involved. A lot of sulking. These days, I'm happy to say, I take a more mature view, but any advice or criticism can still sting a little.

First of all, thank your reader! No matter how you are feeling about it, your beta reader took the time and trouble to read your work and formulate their thoughts on it, and a quick thank you will make sure they know that you appreciate their input.

Remember, feedback on your book is not a criticism of you as a person. Writing is such an individual thing. It takes so much time. We become wrapped up in it and can pour our heart and soul onto the page. If you're not invested in your writing, you are probably not doing it right! However, once you have a manuscript which you are ready to share with other people, you must accept that it is separate from you. Your book is a product of your mind, emotions, labour and love, but now it needs to make its way in the world. Your job is to make it the best it can be and then let it go out and find readers, who will bring their own experience, understanding and mental state to the party. A little while ago, I watched 'You Hurt My Feelings,' a film about the upset within a marriage caused when a writer overhears her husband's honest opinion of her work. Not my favourite film, but it delivered one line which really struck home: *You are not your book.* Please remember this as you take the next steps on your book's journey.

Read through feedback once and then leave it. It may be tempting to rush into edits, but you will be carrying a lot of excess emotion if you do it straight away. Read the comments and then put them aside for a while, at least twenty-four hours. Let yourself calm down and allow the words to settle in your brain. When you come back to them, you will be able to deal with the whole situation more rationally.

When you are ready to go back to the feedback, read it through again and make notes or annotate the online or printed advice. What are the key messages? You might not agree with some of the comments, but at least try to understand why your reader has made them. If you understand where they are coming from, but still don't agree, fair enough. It's your book after all. Consider each point and make a list of things to fix.

I tend to address the small or easy things first (inconsistencies or little plot gaps), then I've got some early wins and ticks on my list. Then I circle back and tackle the big ones.

20.7 BEGINNINGS AND ENDINGS

'The first chapter sells the book; the last chapter sells the next book.'
— Mickey Spillane

Obviously, you want your whole book to be the best it can be, but I would urge you to pay particular attention to the first three chapters, which are the ones a prospective agent or publisher will see. They receive hundreds of submissions every year. Their time is at a premium. Make sure you hook your reader in quickly. Set it out clearly so that it is easy to read (1.5 line spacing, first line of each paragraph indented apart from the first paragraph in each chapter). Don't forget the last chapter, too. These are the words that will create the feeling the reader holds when they finish your book – what do you want them to take away with them?

Once you are happy and confident with your third, fourth, fifth, seventeenth(!), draft, then it is time to consider your options.

20.8 SUGGESTIONS

1. There is power in leaving your book to marinate for a while and coming back to it after a decent gap. I know you want to 'get on with it' but a break *will* be beneficial. Once you have finished your draft, put it away for at least a week.

2. In order to bring fresh eyes to your work, try sending it to your Kindle or other

ereader. Try to approach it as a reader –
not easy, but this is the perspective that you
need now.

3. Read your work out loud. You will notice
   words or passages which jar and dialogue
   that doesn't ring true.

PUBLISHING MODELS

"Publishing is a business. Writing may be art, but publishing, when all is said and done, comes down to dollars."
— Nicholas Sparks

21.1 DIFFERENT PUBLISHING MODELS – WHAT IS RIGHT FOR ME?

Publishing is changing. When I was first published nearly fifteen years ago, there was really only one route – to hope your book would be picked up by a traditional publisher. Most writers had agents, although I found my initial publisher via a local arts festival and didn't have an agent for the first 7 years of my writing career. Nowadays, there are a number of options open to you and to decide which is right for you, you need to work out what is important to you. Do you want the status and prestige that being traditionally published still brings with it? Are you looking for a steady income? Is writing an 'extra' in your life, or do you want it to be your main source of income? How much time can you commit to writing – e.g. can you see yourself writing more than one book a year? While there are three main strands in publishing these days, which I set out below, you don't have to exclusively pursue one type. A hybrid career, combining two or more strands is perfectly possible and may have advantages.

21.1.1 Traditional publisher

For many, a deal with a traditional publisher and then seeing your book produced beautifully and on the shelves of Waterstones is the dream, and it does come true for some. A traditional publisher will:

- Offer a sum of money which is an advance against future sales, usually paid in three parts – on signature, on delivery of an acceptable manuscript, on publication.

- Have a long lead-in time between agreeing a contract and publishing your book (up to two years) which means that it might be a long time before you see you book on the shelf (and even longer before you receive any royalties).
- Have a plan for the publication of different formats. This might include a hardback, paperback, ebook and audiobook.
- Have views on how quickly they might want to publish a second book, which can feel like pressure, if you don't already have a second manuscript up your sleeve.
- Only pay royalties once your book has earned out i.e. receipts from book sales exceed the money paid in advance. Royalties tend to be paid every six months, in arrears. It can seem like a long time to wait for your money!
- Try to place books in bookshops, supermarkets, etc. Increasingly, this is not guaranteed.

- Consider submitting your book to literary prizes – some prizes require the publisher to provide multiple copies or a sum of money to take part.
- Have publicity and marketing professionals who will send out advance copies, look for publicity opportunities, put you forward for literary festivals, etc.
- Take the lead on cover design, blurb, marketing, etc. Publishers vary in how much or little they consult/inform the author on these.

21.1.2 Digital First publisher

A digital first publisher will tend to concentrate on ebooks and digital marketing, but some will do paperbacks and audiobooks. They will:

- Rarely offer an advance but will usually have a better royalty rate for ebooks than a traditional publisher.
- Have shorter lead in times. Your book will probably be available within a year, and it could be a few months.

- Probably be looking to build momentum by publishing two or more books a year. The pace of digital first publishing can be blistering, and only you will know if you can work consistently to produce manuscripts that quickly.
- Pay royalties either quarterly or monthly. Since there is no advance to earn back, royalties will be paid more quickly than with traditional publishing.
- Focus on the ebook but may also include paperbacks and audiobooks. It is less likely for paperbacks from digital first publishers to get into bookstores.
- Take the lead on cover design, blurb, marketing, etc.

21.1.3 Independent publishing

With independent publishing, also known as self-publishing, the author arranges everything and makes key decisions. As an independent author:

- You invest your own time and money in editing, cover design, blurb, etc.

- You decide on the publishing timescale, which can be a lot quicker than either traditional or digital first publisher.
- You control the pace of publishing. Many successful independent writers publish several books a year, but the pace is up to you.
- You decide the marketing spend and strategy.
- You keep a much greater percentage of the receipts (just paying whatever admin fee applies to each platform).
- You are less likely to be eligible for awards or be invited to speak at traditional book festivals. Independent publishing still doesn't have the kudos that traditional publishing does.

21.1.4 Vanity Publishing

A word about vanity publishers. These are businesses who charge authors to publish them. They appear to offer an easy route to publication – you simply provide them with your words and they do the rest. Their whole business model is based on profiting from author fees and self-purchases. The author pays upfront and the fee will cover the costs of production and the company's overheads. They will not be selective about the books they accept, and there may be issues about the quality of editing, design and so on that you receive. Some may also use the label 'hybrid' implying that they are sharing the costs and risks with the author, or appear to be a traditional publisher, but a closer examination of the terms, conditions and fees is necessary here. If you are not sure whether you are dealing with a vanity publisher or not, the website Writer Beware 'shines a bright light into the dark corners of the shadow-world of literary scams, schemes, and pitfalls' and may be worth checking out.

21.2 DO I NEED AN AGENT?

Agents have traditionally been the conduit between writers and publishers. An agent will take a percentage of any income arising from a deal that they broker, typically 15%. Not only do they prepare a submission package and send your work to their editorial contacts within publishing houses, they will also conduct negotiations with interested parties, including holding bidding auctions (the dream!), negotiate any contract terms in the event of an agreed offer, and be your advocate during the life of any contract agreed, should problems arise. In addition to this they may also:

- give you advice about developing a long-term, sustainable career
- have editorial input
- be a good sounding board for new ideas
- pass on enquiries/other writing jobs/opportunities
- sell foreign and media rights

Even before the advent of new business models, an agent wasn't essential. I managed for seven years without one, and only looked for one when I wanted to break into a new genre. With the publishing world rapidly evolving, you certainly don't *have* to have an agent, especially if you are mostly focused on digital-first publishers or independent publishing. If you are interested in netting a traditional publishing deal, though, then a good agent could make a huge difference to your writing career.

If you are aiming for a traditional deal, ask yourself what you want from an agent. They tend to have different styles and strengths and areas of expertise. They will also have different communication styles. Some will offer more editorial help than others. If you know other agented writers, ask for their advice – would they recommend their own agent? Research writers whose books or careers you admire and find out who they are agented by. Have a look at agents' social media activity – you will get an idea about their enthusiasms and style. Consult the Writers' and Artists' Yearbook for a comprehensive list of agents and publishers.

When you have drawn up a list of agents who look like they could be a good match for you, do not send anything to them until:

- You are very confident that your first draft is the best you can make it at this stage
- You have read each agent's submission guidelines
- You have put together a concise and compelling covering letter
- You have written a one-page synopsis
- The sample of the writing that you are sending meets their submission guidelines in terms of format and length.

I have kept this section fairly brief. I could actually write a whole book about it(!) and there is plenty of advice out there if you want to research this further.

21.3 AND BREATHE...

If this all feels overwhelming, take a step back. There is no rush. Take a moment to feel a sense of achievement at having written a book! It really is something worth celebrating. Whatever happens next, no one can take this milestone away from you! You did it!

21.4 EXERCISE

1. Think about what you really want next. What would success look or feel like to you? Write out a bullet point list of what you hope to achieve through writing/publishing, then try and number your points in order of importance. What really matters to you? Your priorities will determine which model of publishing you want to pursue, and whether or not you need an agent.

2 2

FINALLY

'I did it for the pure joy of the thing. And if you can do it for joy, you can do it forever.'
— Stephen King

I hope this book has given you some of the tools you need to write your cozy mystery. Please use it as a resource. Dip back into it if you need some hints, tips or reassurance. Writing is not easy. Even though I've been writing profession-ally for many years, I still get in a muddle, I often hit the 'soggy middle' and wonder how I'll ever get out of it, and I have doubts and dark nights of the soul. I also have the sort of writing day when the words just flow, I sail past my word target and I feel like I'm in exactly the right place, at the right time, doing the right thing. Whether it's a good writing day or a bad one, I love spending time with my cast of characters and I'm excited to write about them and see how they develop. I hope that you, too, find this 'happy place' as you write your cozy mystery. Yes, the outcome is important, but the process is the thing we spend our days doing. As Annie Dillard said, 'How we spend our days is, of course, how we spend our lives. What we do with this hour, and that one, is what we are doing.' I hope that writing, whenever and wherever you do it, is a thing of joy for you.

Whatever advice you read, you will find your own way, and, if you keep going, you *will* be able to tell your story.

REFERENCES

Chapter 2

1. For more information about the author:
   www.rachelward.com

Chapter 4

1. 'Mystery – How To Write Traditional and
   Cozy Whodunnits,' Paul Tomlinson, 2017
2. 'How to Write a Cozy Mystery,' Nina
   Harrington, NinaHarringtonDigital, 2021
3. 'Cosy Crime Novels: Are They Brilliant
   Entertainment or Twee and Insipid?' David
   Barnett, BBC website, 2023
4. 'What The World of Cozy Mysteries Says
   About Violence,' Alyse Burnside, The
   Atlantic, 2021
5. 'A Brief History of Detective Fiction,' Emily
   Martin, Novel Suspects, Hachette Book
   Group online newsletter

Chapter 5

1. 'The Enduring Appeal of Cozy Mysteries',
   post on Crimereads website, 14/08/2023
2. 'UK Book Sales in 2021 Highest in Decade,'
   Alison Flood, The Guardian online, 2022

3. www.alexandermccallsmith.co.uk

Chapter 9

1. 'Save The Cat, The Last Book on Screenwriting You'll Ever Need,' Blake Snyder, Michael Wiese Productions, 2005
2. S.J. Bennett, speaking at Chiltern Kills Crime Festival, 2023

Chapter 10

1. 'Into the Woods', John Yorke, Penguin, 2013
2. 'Save the Cat' as above.
3. 'How to Write a Novel Using the Snowflake Method,' Randy Ingermanson, CreateSpace Independent Publishing Platform, 2014
4. 'Write Your Novel From the Middle,' James Scott Bell, Compendium Press, 2014

Chapter 11

1. Antony Johnston, The Conversation with Nadine Matheson podcast, Episode 50.

Chapter 12

1. Trevor Wood, Why Setting is Important in Crime Fiction, post for Faber Academy website, Why Setting Matters in Crime Writing | Reading Room | Faber Academy, 13/07/23

Chapter 13

1. 'Submission to CMA Call for Information by Digital Task Force,' Bookseller's Association, July 2020
2. 'Tips for Writing in Third Person Point of View,' Masterclass, 2023

Chapter 14

1. Quote from Jessica Bull., author of Miss Austen Investigates, X/Twitter chat #cosycrimeclub, 7/05/24
2. 8 Tips for Writing in Third Person Point of View, 8 Tips for Writing in Third-Person Point of View - 2024 - MasterClass
3. For writing exercises, try Creative Writing Exercises and Prompts

Chapter 16

1. London Writers' Salon, Writers' Hour: London Writers' Salon (londonwriterssalon.com)
2. Yoga with Adriene

Chapter 17

1. 'Just One Thing,' Michael Mosley, BBC Radio 4
2. 'The Artist's Way, a Spiritual Path to Creativity,' Julia Cameron, Tarcherperigee,

2020

Chapter 18

1. Joanna Penn website: The Creative Penn. Writing, Publishing, Book Marketing and Making a Living with your Writing

Chapter 19

1. 'Writers' and Artists' Yearbook 2023: The best advice on how to write and get published,' Bloomsbury Yearbooks, 2022.

FICTION BOOKS REFERENCED

Chapter 2

- Numbers, Rachel Ward.
- The Supermarket Mysteries, Rachel Ward
- The Missing Checkout Girl Mystery
- The Missing Pets Mystery
- The Missing Babysitter Mystery
- The Missing Red Carpet Mystery
- The Missing Heirloom Mystery (2024)

Chapter 3

- The Moonstone, Wilkie Collins

- Sherlock Holmes stories, Sir Arthur Conan Doyle
- Hercule Poirot and Miss Marple books, Agatha Christie
- Lord Peter Wimsey books, Dorothy L. Sayers
- Josephine Tey
- Freeman Wills Croft
- M C Beaton
- The No 1 Ladies Detective Agency, Alexander McCall Smith
- The Thursday Murder Club and The Last Devil to Die, Richard Osman
- The Cat Who... series, Lilian Jackson Braun

Chapter 9

- The Last Dance, Mark Billingham
- The Ruth Galloway series, Elly Griffiths
- The Mothers' Murder Club Mysteries, Kate Ailes
- The Dinner Lady Detectives series, Hannah Hendy
- The Girl Who Vanished, Rachel Ward
- The Dales Detectives series, Julia Chapman

- Her Majesty Investigates series, SJ Bennett
- Baby Ganesh Detective Agency series, Vaseem Khan
- Granchester series, James Runcie
- Charity Shop Detective Agency series, Peter Boland
- Bronte Mysteries series, Bella Ellis
- The Retired Detectives Club series, Steph Broadribb
- The Last Supper, Rosemary Shrager
- Knife Skills for Beginners, Orlando Murrin
- Canon Clement Mysteries, Reverend Richard Coles
- Father Brown series, G.K. Chesterton
- Charles Paris series, Simon Brett
- Danny Bird Mysteries, Derek Farrell
- Honey Driver series, Jean G. Goodhind
- Malvern Farm Mysteries series, Kate Wells
- The Maid, Nita Prose
- Nosey Parker series, Fiona Leitch
- Save The Cat series of writing advice books, Blake Snyder

Chapter 12

- High Rise Mystery, Sharna Jackson
- Miss Austen Investigates, Miss Austen Investigates

Chapter 14

- The Appeal, Janice Hallett
- Pride and Prejudice, Jane Austen

Connect with Rachel Ward

Newsletter: www.cosycrimeclubmore.substack.com

Website: www.rachelwardbooks.com

X/Twitter: @RachelWardbooks

ACKNOWLEDGMENTS

Writing this book has been a passion project, a steep learning curve and an exercise in backing myself. I couldn't have done it without a lot of help and I'm grateful to every single person who encouraged me along the way, including:

Debbie Picken at RetreatsForYou for inviting me to run a cozy mystery writing retreat in September 2023, which started this whole idea rolling.

Joanna Penn for inspiring me to seize the initiative and share what I've learned.

The writing buddies who I spend time with in real life and online, especially Emma Pass and Sheena Wilkinson, members of the Place, London Writers' Salon's Writers' Hour, and so many others, including Leila Rashid, Sophia Bennett, Liz Kessler, Lynne Benton, Orlando Murrin, Derek O'Farell, and Colin Scott.

Authors who have been special guests at my X/Twitter chat #cosycrimeclub, plus the other writers and readers who meet there to discuss their favourite books and what makes them so special.

Ed James for help with formatting.

Steve Wells for cover design.

Alison Ward for website advice and all-round tech support.

Peter Ward for life coaching and commonsense.

Andrew Ward for being the best sounding board ever, beta reader, ideas generator and all-round good egg.